GLOME PF

THE
RETURN
OF THE DRAGON

The Shocking Way Drugs and Religion Shape People and Societies

LEWIS UNGIT

Glome is a locally focused publishing company.

Printed in the United States of America

First Printing 2022

ISBN: 9798846138698

Glome Press

LewisUngit.Substack.Com

Cover and Design by Lewis Ungit

Table of Contents

To Joe and John.

I
Pandora's Box

As a wedding gift, Zeus gave Pandora a box — but he warned her never to open it. However, Pandora was incurably curious and couldn't stop thinking about it. Finally, overwhelmed with the desire to find out what was inside, she peeked. But as so often happens when we ignore warnings, Pandora immediately regretted her action. Out from the box came curses the world had hitherto not known: greed, envy, hatred, pain, disease, hunger, poverty, war, and death. Pandora's decision to ignore the warnings of Zeus led to untold miseries being poured out into the world. Pandora slammed the lid of the box back down but it was too late.

The story of Pandora has provided a template for many western myths and fictional stories. Even in today's culture, everyone knows that when you are watching a movie about an adventurous archeologist encountering a long-lost tomb, if he sees a sign that says, "Whoever opens this door will be cursed," bad things are in store if he chooses to go forward.

Of course, this pattern is not just found in myths, novels, and action movies. We tell ourselves these stories because all too often we need to be reminded that sometimes there are truly dangerous things that really will bring destruction if warnings are ignored.

There's another ancient myth that has a similar theme to it. We find it at the beginning of the biblical book of Genesis:

> "Now the serpent was more subtle than any beast of the field which the Lord God had made. And he said unto the woman, "Yea, hath God said, ye shall not eat of every tree of the garden?"
>
> And the woman said unto the serpent, "We may eat of the fruit of the trees of the garden: But of the fruit of the tree which is in the midst of the garden, God hath said, Ye shall not eat of it, neither shall ye touch it, lest ye die."
>
> And the serpent said unto the woman, "Ye shall not surely die: For God doth know that in the day ye eat thereof, then your eyes shall be opened, and ye shall be as gods, knowing good and evil"

And when the woman saw that the tree was good for food and that it was pleasant to the eyes, and a tree to be desired to make one wise, she took of the fruit thereof, and did eat, and gave also unto her husband with her; and he did eat." (Genesis 3:1-6)

Here we see a similar pattern to Pandora. A God warns a woman not to do something. But in this story, unlike in Pandora's, a serpent appears. This serpent appeals to the curiosity of the woman. What would happen if she disobeyed God?

According to Christian and Jewish traditions, the woman's decision to listen to the serpent and eat the fruit brought all kinds of evil into the world. The acceptance of this story as historical was once so common that the great Isaac Newton even considered it to be a literal account of events that happened roughly 6,000 years ago. But over the past few centuries, evolutionary scientists, paleontologists, and archeologists have come to maintain that humanity and the world are much older. Humanity in our present form, they say, is at least 100,000 years old and the world itself is millions of years old. And, needless to say, science also tells us that serpents do not talk. And so the story of Eve, Adam, and the serpent has shifted in western consciousness from a story of history to a story of myth.

Well…

What if we learned that sometimes serpents do talk? What if we found sane and honest people in the modern world who would testify that they have indeed spoken with serpents? And what if there really is a forbidden fruit that brings horrors into the world? If we found these things to be true, how would that change our understanding of the story found in the book of Genesis?

A few years ago, I heard about a drug called DMT (the abbreviation for the chemical dimethyltryptamine). What I heard sounded fantastical and impossible. People who took the drug all experienced the same things: they saw geometric shapes (not unlike those found in ancient Mesoamerican art) and they met entities. These entities were often described as machine elves or aliens. Some called them demons. Some called them angels. But the entities were experienced universally. Mystical hippies taking the drug to expand their consciousness experienced them. Hyper-skeptical Western atheists experienced them. People from obscure tribes experienced them.

I read a bit about DMT at the time and then I moved on to other interests. But the subject seemed to keep coming into my field of consciousness. I read a book called *America Before,* by Graham Hancock, in which he discussed his own experiences on DMT. I listened to the Joe Rogan Experience podcast and he talked glowingly about his experiences on DMT. I read a magazine article about Silicon Valley tech executives taking small doses of DMT as a way of gaining creativity. And with each of these, my interest grew. What was DMT? Why did people always experience the same things? What exactly were they experiencing?

It was then that I went fully down the rabbit hole. I read everything I could find on the subject of DMT, and the reading caused me to open up my interest to hallucinogenic drugs as a whole (including others like LSD, magic mushrooms, and marijuana). The more I read, the more convinced I became that there was something we were all missing. Something deeper and more real than simple hallucinations.

This book is the result of my findings.

II
Reemergence

Recently I was walking near my home and saw a long line of middle-aged people with greasy unwashed hair, dirty old concert t-shirts, old hoodies, sweat pants, and frayed pajama pants. The line circled the block and led up to a house. Based on the rough look of the crowd, I wondered if a grunge band from the 1990s was doing a house concert. But it was Sunday morning so I asked one of them, "What are you waiting in line for?"

"Weed," the man in a faded Metallica shirt replied.

And then I remembered. A law legalizing the recreational use and sale of marijuana had just gone into effect. The line was for one of the state's first pot dispensaries. Michigan is one of many states that have legalized marijuana over the past decade. It is a trend that shows no sign of stopping.

Twenty years ago, marijuana was illegal everywhere. What changed?

Almost everyone decided that marijuana is no big deal. Culturally it became normal — what was once taboo slowly became socially acceptable. Many wondered why it had been illegal in the first place.

A 2021 Pew Research Center report stated that Americans now overwhelmingly support legalizing marijuana for recreational or for medical use. The survey found, "an overwhelming share of U.S. adults (91%) say either that marijuana should be legal for medical and recreational use (60%) or that it should be legal for medical use only (31%). Fewer than one in ten (8%) say marijuana should not be legal for use by adults."[1]

It is as though as a nation we all agreed together that this substance was not a threat. We all asked, "Why was marijuana illegal? What was the problem with it?"

And many are now asking the same questions about other non-addictive psychotropic drugs. People understand why drugs that destroy health and create hardcore debilitating addictions are wrong, but what about lysergic acid diethylamide (LSD), psilocybin (magic mushrooms), peyote, and ayahuasca (DMT)? None of these are addictive, and there are very few known negative side effects (at least when taken in reasonable doses).

---

[1] Green, 2021.

And so, just as we did with marijuana, there is now a cultural conversation about these psychedelic drugs. Why are they illegal? What is wrong with them?

In November 2020, Oregon became the first U.S. state to decriminalize possession of small amounts of LSD.[2] There is a push to legalize LSD in California.[3] And political pundits speculate this is just the start of psychedelics following marijuana's path to legalization.[4]

But, unlike with Marijuana, there is another question about these drugs that is being asked: what are the positive benefits? Can these once-taboo drugs help us emotionally and spiritually?

And increasingly, leaders in both culture and academia have agreed that the answer is yes. As we will see below, influential thinkers in culture and academia have very high hopes for the use of these psychedelics and how they can improve, cure, and enlighten society.

One of the most outspoken voices promoting the reintroduction of psychedelics into society is bestselling author Graham Hancock. Hancock is an alternative historian who has made a career out of questioning traditional historical narratives. He has written extensively on ancient Mesoamerica, arguing that the Americas were

---

[2] Feuer, 2020.
[3] Jaeger, 2021.
[4] Zhang & Campton, 2022.

settled far earlier than traditional scholars have believed, and that the people who settled them were far more technologically advanced than anyone could imagine. But he also writes about the drugs that the Mesoamericans took as part of their religion, and considers this one of the keys to how they were able to achieve great things. He wrote a book, *Supernatural,* specifically talking about a particular Mesoamerican drug, ayahuasca, the active ingredient of which is dimethyltryptamine (often abbreviated to DMT). Graham is widely read, is a large force on social media, and is a favorite guest of podcasters.

Hancock's discussions on psychedelics (and ayahuasca in particular) are compelling, interesting, and convincing. He says, "I am here to attest that in several (though by no means all) of my many ayahuasca sessions I have been blessed with experiences of such extraordinary power, yielding such penetrating insights, that I unhesitatingly rank them among the most powerful of my life."[5]

Joe Rogan, with his insanely popular podcast, has brought the use of psychedelic drugs out of the hippie subculture and obscure corners of society and into the mainstream. He regularly talks about ayahuasca and psilocybin (the synthetic version of "magic mushrooms") and the spiritual and mental benefits he attributes to them. His shows have featured Graham Hancock and other

---

[5] Muraresku, xvii.

advocates of psychedelics. Rogan recommends psychedelics and notes that "Maybe [DMT] will make you a better person."[6]

Another bestselling author who has done much to promote the reintroduction of psychedelics into American culture is Michael Pollan. In his book, *How to Change Your Mind*, he lays out the case that psychedelics provide mental, emotional, and societal benefits.

Recounting one person's experience, he writes,

> *"Mushrooms have taught me the interconnectedness of all life-forms and the molecular matrix that we share...I no longer feel that I am in this envelope of a human life ... I am part of the stream of molecules that are flowing through nature. I am given a voice, given consciousness for a time, but I feel that I am part of this continuum of stardust into which I am born and to which I will return at the end of this life."[7]*

Pollan compiled data and anecdotes detailing how meaningful and moving the experience of taking psychedelics is to the people that do. He writes,

> *"Participants ranked their psilocybin experience as one of the most meaningful in their lives, comparable 'to the birth of a first child or death of a parent.' Two-*

[6] Joe Rogan Experience Podcast #1543.
[7] Pollan, 125.

thirds of the participants rated the session among the top five 'most spiritually significant experiences' of their lives; one-third ranked it the most significant such experience in their lives."[8]

Other influential podcasters such as Lex Fridman have made similar statements (with Fridman recently dedicating a whole episode to the benefits of psychedelics). He said, "There is something to the opening up of creativity whether it is for writing purposes… or engineering and invention…. It is fascinating to think that with the aid of psychedelics what kind of ideas can be brought to life."[9]

And this movement is not limited to the social or political left as it was in the 1960s. Right-leaning filmmaker, author, and Twitter celebrity, Mike Cernovich, recently wrote, "I'm not interested in the political insights of people who haven't journeyed on ayahuasca."[10] Elsewhere he wrote, "ayahuasca heals minds."[11]

In addition to popular authors and podcasters, there has been a movement within the Silicon Valley Tech World to use psychedelics as a means of developing insights and creativity. Pollan has an excellent discussion on how the tech world used drugs to gain insights and help creativity. He says,

---

[8] Pollan, 11.
[9] Rick Doblin: Psychedelics | LexFridman Podcast #202.
[10] Tweet, February 2, 2021.
[11] Tweet March 29,2021

"Schwartz said that several of the early computer engineers relied on LSD in designing circuit chips, especially in the years before they could be designed on computers. "You had to be able to visualize a staggering complexity in three dimensions, hold it all in your head. They found that LSD could help."[12]

Later he writes, "I know of one Bay Area tech company today that uses psychedelics in its management training."[13]

This growing cultural acceptance parallels the growing interest found in the halls of academia.

Increasingly LSD and psilocybin are being studied as potential treatments for a variety of mental disorders. The New York Times summarized the growing enthusiasm with this 2021 headline: "The Psychedelic Revolution Is Coming. Psychiatry May Never Be the Same."[14]These sentiments result from an increasingly large number of trials at major universities. Universities like Johns Hopkins, New York University, and the University of Wisconsin- Madison have all conducted studies that indicated promising results. We will review some of these studies in the next chapter, but their findings are fascinating. Academics are expressing growing confidence that psychedelics may offer relief to a variety of mental conditions and addictions.

---

[12] Pollan, 177.
[13] Pollan, 177.
[14] Jacobs, 2021.

And so, with growing acceptance within the cultural, business, and academic worlds, we are seeing a shift similar to that which we saw with marijuana. We have begun to change our minds on psychedelics. We have gone from viewing them as something scary to seeing them as a potentially good thing.

But what this book asks is the question: Why did we ban psychotropic drugs in the first place? Was it a quirk of history? A Victorian eccentricity? Should we view the warnings of generations past as irrelevant and retrograde? Or are those warnings like the warning of Zeus to Pandora?

Before we dive into the history of why these drugs were banned in the first place, let's examine the experiences of people on psychedelics. Let's look at what they see, hear, feel, and encounter and how the drugs affect their life after they come down from their highs.

III
Experiences

I remember when I first took mushrooms. I sat in a dark room lit by blacklights and decorated with Led Zeppelin posters. The musty smell of cigarettes and cheap wine went unnoticed as the three of us sat on a saggy plaid couch. After we had all choked down two or three mushrooms and gagged slightly from the taste, my friend Ricardo stood up, turned on Pink Floyd's classic double album, *The Wall*, and we all sat back and melted into the universe.

It was a shabby atmosphere for the event that many describe as life-changing, but my experience was as powerful as others have described it. It felt meaningful. It felt important. It felt transcendent. Psychedelic trips are notoriously hard to convey outside of the experience, and mine was no exception. The only thing I could communicate afterward was that it showed me that what we see is only a tiny percentage of what is. In retrospect, I did not walk away from the trip with some renewed understanding of the universe or any new moral insights, but at the time I felt as though I had figured everything out.

I tripped several times after that (taking LSD, and Mescaline on various occasions). But I soon found I didn't like the effect it had on me. I felt as though it was drawing me away from reality, pulling me out of this world and making me less grounded. I consciously decided that tripping was bad for my brain and bad for my soul. I even quit pot from that point forward.

But for every person with a story like mine, I have heard others describe their takeaways as much more transformative. In Michael Pollan's *How to Change Your Mind*, he gives many anecdotes of people who took LSD or psilocybin and were completely changed. And we can all think of famed authors and celebrities who talk about their psychedelic experiences as some of the most important in their lives.

So what is the psychedelic experience like? What are the subjective and objective effects of taking psychedelics? The purpose of this chapter is to survey some of the landscape of the experiences of people while on psychedelics and talk about what advocates claim are their greatest benefits.

Spiritual experiences

Michael Pollan speaks of the fact that psychedelic experiences have a necessary spiritual effect on the user. He writes:

> *"You go deep enough or far out enough in consciousness and you will bump into the sacred. It's not something we generate; it's something out there waiting to be discovered. And this reliably happens to nonbelievers as well as believers."*[15]

Something out there? What is out there? This statement by Pollan directly reflects my own experience. And it is also reflected in the psychedelic experiences of everyone I have known to use LSD or magic mushrooms.

Later he expresses agreement with the views of psychedelic researcher Bob Jesse, who considered the simple medicalization of psychedelics to be a mistake because he *"was ultimately less interested in people's mental problems than with their spiritual well-being."*[16]

A Johns Hopkins study which we will discuss in more depth later in this chapter found psilocybin had profound spiritual effects even on atheists. The study states, "Twenty-one percent of the psychedelic users reported

---

[15] Pollan, 55.
[16] Pollan, 51.

being atheists before their experience, while only 8 percent reported being atheists after."[17] As Pollan summarizes it, "The Johns Hopkins experiment shows—proves—that under controlled, experimental conditions, psilocybin can occasion genuine mystical experiences."[18]

There is something deeply spiritual about taking psychedelics. Some sort of existential understanding. Some sort of profound and ineffable communion. In my conversations with people who enjoy "tripping," this is the thing that gets them to keep doing it. They feel they are communing in some way with God, gods, spirits, or the universe as a whole. It is a profound and spiritual experience that they seek.

Geometric Shapes

Dr. Rick Strassman, a Professor of Psychiatry at the University of New Mexico School of Medicine, led a study published by the American Medical Association which found that participants in a study on DMT saw dramatic geometric shapes and kaleidoscope-like colors.[19]This is another one of the most common experiences that people report as they take various psychedelics, and ayahuasca in particular. Geometric patterns — often described as

---

[17] Griffiths, 2019.
[18] Pollan, 81.
[19] Strassman, 1994.

being like ancient Mesoamerican art— such as zigzags and stepped lines overwhelm the participant.

Consider Graham Hancock's experience on ayahuasca:

> "*Very often these luminous designs, rich in data, take the form of geometry. … [upon consuming ayahuasca] without fanfare a parade of visions suddenly begins, visions that are at once geometrical and alive, visions of lights unlike any light I've ever seen—dark lights, a pulsing, swirling field of the deepest luminescent violets, of reds emerging out of the night, of unearthly textures and colors, of solar systems revolving, of spiral galaxies on the move. Visions of nets and strange ladder-like structures… .a recurrence of the geometrical patterns…a background of shifting geometrical patterns… complex interlaced patterns of geometry.… I zoom in for a closer view.… They're rectangular, outlined in black, like windows. There's a circle in the centre of each rectangle.*"[20]

Hancock even speculates that these geometric shapes that are seen while on ayahuasca might in part explain the amazing parallels in art and architecture across disparate cultures around the globe and throughout the ages.[21]

---

[20] Hancock, America Before: The Key to Earth's Lost Civilization, 2019, 221.
[21] Hancock, America Before: The Key to Earth's Lost Civilization, 2019, 349.

Entities

In addition to having spiritual experiences and seeing what is often described as delightful and awe-inspiring geometry, users of psychedelics also report interacting with entities. This is especially true of those who take ayahuasca or DMT. They drink the brew and suddenly they find themselves in the presence of other beings or entities. In his study, conducted in the 1980s and 1990s, Strassman aimed to examine the effects of DMT and to document the experiences of 60 volunteers. When he published his research in *DMT: The Spirit Molecule*, he reported that half the volunteers encountered humanoid or animal entities.[22][23]

While some of the things people see while on DMT can be considered culturally conditioned, the surprising finding in studies of the drug is that many experiences are common across all cultures. As University of Greenwich's David Luke says,

> *"[There] are uncanny commonalities at the core of experiences emanating from old folkloric accounts of fairies; anthropological and indeed firsthand accounts from indigenous cultures; as well as from FDA-approved experimental research; so-called*

---

[22] Strassman R. , 2000.
[23] Charbonneau, Jason.

"recreational" and maybe even biblical DMT trip reports; and even alien abduction cases."[24]

I spent quite a bit of time reading first-person accounts from participants in studies and from those who simply took ayahuasca for personal reasons. The accounts are riveting and compelling. Consider this statement from one user:

> *"When I was first going under there were these insect creatures all around me. They were clearly trying to break through. I was fighting letting go of who I am or was. The more I fought, the more demonic they became, probing into my psyche and being."*[25]

Another DMT user describes an experience with other entities,

> *"There were a lot of elves. They were prankish, [and] ornery, maybe four of them appeared at the side of a stretch of interstate highway I travel regularly. They commanded the scene, it was their terrain! They were about my height. They held up placards, showing me these incredibly beautiful, complex, swirling geometric scenes in them. One of them made it impossible for me to move. There was no issue of control; they were*

---

[24] Luke, What We Think We Know About DMT Entities, 2018, 299.
[25] Razer, 2021.

totally in control. They wanted me to look! I heard a giggling sound — the elves laughing or talking at high-speed volume, chattering, twittering.[26]

The encounters above showed entities that were scary or at least tricky but most entities observed are experienced as benevolent. Consider this statement from a study published in the Journal of Psychopharmacology,

> *"The most common descriptive labels for the entity were being, guide, spirit, alien, and helper. Although 41% of respondents reported fear during the encounter, the most prominent emotions both in the respondent and attributed to the entity were love, kindness, and joy. Most respondents endorsed that the entity had the attributes of being conscious, intelligent, and benevolent, existed in some real but different dimension of reality, and continued to exist after the encounter."*[27]

The frequency in which people see entities that look like animals, people, and people animal hybrids is very interesting. Those who have seen these entities often note the similarities between the visions they see and the art of ancient indigenous people around the world. The gods and goddesses of old found in caves, in tombs, in temples, and

---

[26] Razer, 2021.
[27] Davis, Clifton, Weaver, Hurwitz, & Johnson, 2020.

in pyramids bear striking a resemblance to the things that people report seeing while on DMT and other powerful hallucinogens.

Overlap Between the Psychedelic and Natural Experiences

The mystical experiences reported by those on psychedelics are also infrequently found among some who have not taken any sort of hallucinogen. Many have noted the interesting overlap between those consuming psychedelics and the accounts of religious mystics who did not take any drugs whatsoever. The mystics use similar language, experience visions of geometric shapes (note how many times in the Bible the prophets start describing geometry that God revealed to them), have similar spiritual experiences, and see entities (saints, angels, demons, etc). Often they come back with prophetic statements about life, meaning, purpose, and God that echo the sorts of confident statements made by users of psychedelics.

And there are physical exercises that can be used to induce these experiences as well. Many have reported that Buddhist meditation and breathing exercises can evoke them. Those skilled in the art of meditation report a loss of self, an oneness with the universe, out-of-body experiences, and other experiences overlapping with the psychedelic. The Journal of Neuroscience reports that some forms of meditation produce changes to the brain which reflect an "endogenous, self-induced high entropy state."[28]

Others report psychedelic experiences while creating and listening to musical rhythms. Rhythmic dancing, drumming, and sometimes simply listening to music can produce altered states of consciousness. A study conducted by researchers at the University of Michigan found that people practicing musical shamanic rituals without the use of drugs experienced "altered states of consciousness" and "in consciousness have overlapping phenomenological traits" to those who take psychedelics. [29]

People also appear to have strikingly similar sensations during near-death experiences. Often people will report being out of body, seeing visions of entities, and gleaning profound spiritual insights. It is so similar to the DMT experience that some have speculated that a small amount of DMT present in all human brains is activated when we approach death.[30][31]

Finally, at least some forms of mental illness appear to give visions similar to the mystical adventures of psychedelics. "Mental health professionals know well," writes William Richards, "that similar experiences [to those of healthy people on psychedelics] usually called

[28] Vivot, Pallavicini, Zamberlan, Vigo, & Tagliazucchi, 2020.
[29] Huels, et al., 2021.
[30] Jaekl, 2018.
[31] Timmermann, et al., 2018.

hallucinations, are reported by distressed people who we often give the diagnosis of the schizophrenia or bipolar disorder..."[32]

In short, the amazing feelings, visions, and insights people report having while on hallucinogens are not solely found through the use of drugs. In a variety of natural states, humans have reported very similar experiences to that of the user of psychedelics. As Graham Hancock writes,

> *"Shamanism is not confined to specific socio-economic settings or stages of development. It is fundamentally the ability that all of us share, some with and some without the help of hallucinogens, to enter altered states of consciousness and to travel out of body in non-physical realms - there to encounter supernatural entities and gain useful knowledge and healing powers from them."[33]*

Out of Body Experiences and Telepathy?

One of the more shocking claims made by users of psychedelics is that they enable paranormal phenomena. While this assertion gets dismissed quickly by those of a more materialistic perspective, testimonies of paranormal happenings are widely reported by users of ayahuasca.[34]

[32] Richards, 2018, 95.
[33] Hancock, Visionary: The Mysterious Origins of Human Consciousness (The Definitive Edition of Supernatural), 2022, 451.
[34] Luke, 2022.

Consider this quote from Benny Shanon, Professor of Psychology at The Hebrew University in Jerusalem,

> *"Practically everyone who has had more than a rudimentary exposure to [ayahuasca] reports having had telepathic experiences. Many such reports also appear in the anthropological literature... Similarly, many of my informants said that without overt verbal articulation they could pass messages to other people present in the ayahuasca session...Likewise, many indicated that they received such messages from other persons or beings. Usually, in visions in which drinkers feel that they are receiving messages or instructions from beings and creatures, the communication in question is said to be achieved without words — directly from thought to thought."*[35]

A recent interview study showed that of 40 users of psychedelic drugs, 40 percent reported some sort of telepathic experience. These included the ability to mentally communicate via images and words, the ability to directly exchange feeling-states, and a dissolution of self where one participant would become one in thought and feeling with a partner. The telepathic sensation was so powerful that "some participants complained about the lack of privacy ...and were hesitant to repeat the

---

[35] Shanon, 2002, pages 256-257.

experience." [36] The feeling is so strong that ayahuasca is alternatively known as "Telepathine".[37]

Sometimes people on hallucinogens report that sober people around them can see or hear phenomena they witness while tripping. One DMT user reported that while on the drug he saw a "harlequin-esque" entity and then the next day his perfectly sober roommate woke him up screaming about seeing a similar entity in her bedroom.[38]

Another otherworldly encounter is that of the so-called out-of-body experience. In Jean Houston and Robert Masters' *The Varieties of Psychedelic Experience: The Classic Guide to the Effects of LSD on the Human Psyche*, the authors note,

> "There is also a fairly common experience where the subject seems to himself to project his consciousness away from his body and then is able to see his body as if he were standing off to one side of it or looking down on it from above. A few subjects feel that they are able to leave the 'material body' and move about in something like the 'astral body' familiar to occultists…The perception of the aura by psychedelic subjects is very common."[39]

---

[36] Johnstad, 2020.
[37] Hancock, America Before: The Key to Earth's Lost Civilization, 2019, 476.
[38] DMT Entities, DMT Times, 2019.
[39] Houston & Masters, 2000.

Skeptics will doubt these claims and confidently state that something else must be going on, but it's without question that many participants tell the stories. It's also without question that stories like this are as old as mankind. Every culture has stories of entities that can appear and disappear. Every culture has stories of beings that can move like spirits outside the body. Every culture has accounts with amazing parallels to these claims of modern users of psychedelics.

Materialistic Explanations?

Most science has a materialistic and somewhat atheistic bias. Spiritual encounters, heavenly geometries, entities, and even paranormal experiences are viewed with curiosity by science, but hardly taken as reflections of reality beyond the brains of those participating in the studies.

Science has used brain studies and scans to study the brain as participants consume psychedelic drugs. In *How to Change Your Mind,* Pollan included almost a full chapter outlining what science knows about what is going on in the brain while humans trip on drugs. He states that brain science has shown that chemicals like lysergic acid diethylamide (LSD) and psilocybin have been shown to disrupt the normal workings of the brain. He writes,

> *"The mystical experience may just be what it feels like when you deactivate the brain's default mode*

network. This can be achieved any number of ways: through psychedelics and meditation... but perhaps also by means of certain breathing exercises, sensory deprivation, fasting, prayer, overwhelming experiences, awe, extreme sports, near-death experiences, and so on."[40]

But whatever insights neuroscience might give us about what is going on in the brain, it is important to realize that the observation of changes in the brain is not actually an explanation of what is being seen and experienced. Stating that deactivating our brain's default mode network causes the mystical experience is not much more explanatory than saying, "taking magic mushrooms causes the mystical experience." It explains a mechanism but is not a satisfying explanation for the experience itself. Nor does it say anything of the truth or falsehood of the experience. It simply notes that when we are having those mystical experiences, there is a certain neural behavior taking place in our brains.

To see how pointing to a mechanism doesn't give insight into the reality of what the mechanism reveals, consider ear wax medicine. We put drops in our ears (a mechanism) and as a result, we can hear things we otherwise could not hear. Does that make the things we hear a hallucination resulting

---

[40] Pollan, 306.

from the medicine? Or consider a recent study regarding age-related macular degeneration. People suffering from the ailment who took atorvastatin experienced significantly improved vision. Are the additional things these patients can see not real?

In both cases, the question is rhetorical because the things they can now hear and see thanks to the medicines they took were things the rest of us can hear and see clearly without medicine. But if we all suffered from macular degeneration and bad earwax, perhaps the question would not be as rhetorical. If psychedelics change something in our brains that allows us to access something that others cannot, this in no way proves that the things being seen, heard, and felt are not "real." Further, it fails to address the more mysterious claims of many users. It fails to account for why so many people (across time and culture) see and hear such similar things (e.g. heavenly geometry, spirits, machine elves, demons, entities, etc) and it certainly fails to explain the paranormal claims of out-of-body experiences, and astral projections.[41]

But perhaps most fatal to any skeptical materialistic explanation from neuroscience is that science can't "see" consciousness. Atheist neuroscientist Sam Harris and his wife, author Annaka Harris, recently discussed consciousness

---

[41] It is not strange for different cultures to interpret entities in light of their cultural context but that they see the entities is amazingly universal.

together on a podcast. They talked about the fact that consciousness is ultimately unobservable to science.[42][43] If this outspoken atheistic neuroscientist admits the opacity of consciousness to science, how in the world can we then claim that neuroscience can explain a particular experience of consciousness?

Another damning challenge to atheistic and naturalistic skeptical explanations is that even atheists cease being skeptical after having first-hand experiences. In fact, when atheists take psychedelics, they often cease to be atheists. As we saw, researchers at the Johns Hopkins University School of Medicine showed that a majority of atheists who took DMT became convinced that there is more to this life than the material world.[44] If the scientific method is built on personal observations, it is not insignificant that those who personally observe the psychedelic world often dismiss atheistic explanations. So we cannot discard what people experience with purely atheistic answers. Atheistic explanations are severely lacking when it comes to consciousness, and even more so when reviewing specific experiences.

Do They Work?

One reason that psychedelics have been used throughout history and continue to spark interest today is that those

---

[42] Harris, 2019.
[43] To learn more about the problem consciousness poses to naturalism see *Appendix 2*.
[44] Hess, 2019.

who partake report real benefits. Is this true? The short answer is, yes. Even applying the lens of modern science, we find that psychedelics have the potential to provide genuine benefits in a variety of areas. Paul Hutson, a professor at the University of Wisconsin-Madison who studies psilocybin and leads the school's center for psychedelics research, says that thanks to the various promising medicinal uses of psychedelics he anticipates there will soon be enough evidence for the Food and Drug Administration (FDA) to approve psilocybin for the treatment of some medical issues by the end of the decade.[45]

Major studies at respected institutions have shown quantifiable benefits to people who are depressed, substance-addicted, neurotic, or anxious. And some of the world's most successful entrepreneurs have noted true improvements in creativity and problem-solving after using psychedelics.

Johns Hopkins and New York University joined ranks to study the use of psilocybin in terminal cancer patients. The study used psilocybin in an effort to help prepare patients for the trauma of a potentially terminal cancer. In the study, 80 percent or more of patients demonstrated clinically significant reductions in standard measures of anxiety and depression.[46] Thirty "hallucinogen-naïve" participants

---

[45] Eschner, 2022.
[46] Pollan, 349.

received orally administered psilocybin, and researchers at Johns Hopkins found that:

> "Psilocybin produced a range of acute perceptual changes, subjective experiences, and labile moods including anxiety. Psilocybin also increased measures of mystical experience. At two months, the volunteers rated the psilocybin experience as having substantial personal meaning and spiritual significance and attributed to the experience sustained positive changes in attitudes and behavior consistent with changes rated by community observers."[47]

In other words, the study showed a reduction in anxiety and an increase in a sense of meaning and significance.

Hallucinogens also show promise in helping with various addictions. A Johns Hopkins study on smokers found that 80 percent of volunteers who had used psilocybin during anti-smoking therapy had remained abstinent after six months.[48] Thousands of alcoholics were treated with LSD and other psychedelics in the 1950s and 1960s, and the results were significant enough to become a standard component of care in areas of Canada before the crackdown in the mid-1960s ended such efforts.[49] A 2012 meta-analysis combining data from the six best randomized controlled

---

[47] Griffiths, 2006.
[48] Pollan, 361.
[49] Pollan, 368.

studies done in this era found statically robust benefits in the treatment of alcohol addiction.[50]

Imperial College, in a 2016 study, administered psilocybin to a group of six men and six women with symptoms of depression. After a week, all of the patients reported improvements. While the effects appear to have faded over time, even the short-term respite was reported by the volunteers to be useful and precious.[51]

Pollan writes, "In recent years, 'psychiatry has gone from being brainless to being mindless,' as one psychoanalyst has put it. If psychedelic therapy proves successful, it will be because it succeeds in rejoining the brain and the mind in the practice of psychotherapy. At least that's the promise."[52]

And while academic studies have shown other benefits for those struggling with disorders, proponents also claim psychedelics benefit the healthy. Many smart, happy, and well-adjusted people report that psychedelics have helped them with creativity and problem-solving.

During the 1960s and 1970s, an organization called the International Foundation for Advanced Study conducted studies to determine if LSD could enhance creativity and problem-solving. They administered doses to engineers, architects, and scientists who were somehow "stuck" in their

---

[50] Pollan, 369.
[51] Pollan, 381.
[52] Pollan, 335.

work on a particular project. Subjects reported increased abilities to visualize problems and determine solutions. And while this study is not as scientifically rigorous as one might hope, it certainly matches anecdotal accounts with figures no less than Silicon Valley titans Steve Jobs and Bill Gates reporting LSD's use and benefits. Countless artists and musicians have reported the same.

Proponents also claim that psychedelics can provide moral improvements to users. From the study in the Journal of Psychopharmacology, we see that,

> *"The experiences were rated as among the most meaningful, spiritual, and psychologically insightful lifetime experiences, with persisting positive changes in life satisfaction, purpose, and meaning attributed to the experiences."*[53]

Some writers, seeing these claimed benefits, become almost hyperbolic with praise for the potential of psychedelics. For example, Brian Muraresku, an author who has written on the history of psychedelics in the west, openly speculates that the banning of psychedelics might be leading the world to destruction.[54]Counter culture author and artist, Gregory Sams, speculates, "Could psychedelics save the world?" noting how they help humanity to live in

---

[53] Davis, Clifton, Weaver, Hurwitz, & Johnson, 2020.
[54] Muraresku, 2020, 71-72.

harmony with the environment.[55] And, as previously noted, Mike Cernovich argues that DMT should be a prerequisite for discussions on politics. [56]

There are many voices both in academia and in popular culture that assert moral and spiritual benefits that flow from the use of psychedelics. But before embracing psychedelics a few questions need to be asked. First, what is it that people are experiencing? If, as we saw above, skeptical dismissals of psychedelic experiences as "all in the head" are problematic, what is the alternative? The next few chapters may get a bit weird as we look at what quantum mechanics, philosophy, and religion might tell us about potential answers. If it is not possible that the experiences can be dismissed as "all in the heads" of the participants, then the investigation as to what is going on must leave the inside of the heads of study participants and look at the broader world for answers.

---

[55] Hancock G. , The Divine Spark: a Graham Hancock Reader: Psychedelics, Consciousness, and the Birth of Civilization, 2015, 304.
[56] "I won't endorse any political candidate who hasn't journeyed with ayahuasca. Tired of soulless, boring pieces of card board." Tweet, July 1, 2021.

IV
Dimensions

When I was a teenager, I fell asleep with a CD playing on repeat. I drifted off to sleep listening to the music. I faded into the dream world. Then I awoke to someone laughing in my room. I sat up and to my horror, there was a girl standing in the shadows of the corner of the bedroom. I recoiled, pushing myself up against the headboard of the bed. But as I breathed and my eyes adjusted I realized that the laughing had been coming from one of the songs on the CD and that the girl in the corner had been my mind making sense of the pattern of shadows combined with the laughing. My heart rate slowed. I was very glad. I reminded myself that, thankfully, ghosts are not real.

There is something very reassuring about living in the three dimensions we can see (four if you count time). Whether we are talking about ghosts or religious beings like angels and demons, there is something disorienting about discussions of the spiritual world. Debates about metaphysics often seem too otherworldly and too speculative to be of value. When we talk of demons, angels, and gods, we tend to think of things that are outside of the natural world. And while we might theoretically believe in them, depending on our religious tradition, we feel quite separate from them and do not really have a definition for what "spiritual" means. This may be why many, while perhaps not officially labeling themselves atheists, prefer to view such discussions as relevant only to what happens when we die — if at all.

But in Chapter 3 we saw that, when atheists take psychedelics, they often cease to be atheists. We saw that they reported experiences that convinced them that there is more to this universe than the three-dimensions we see. These people who are not *spiritual*— and who in fact reject the existence of the spiritual — take psychedelics, and then get a glimpse of a world that convinces them there is more than what their material assumptions have led them to believe. Sometimes these former atheists join traditional religions, but often they simply adopt an informal spirituality. The experiential evidence is enough for them to discard a previously held naturalistic view of the universe in favor of something that looks more religious to outsiders.

So here we have a rare case where the two worlds col-lide; no longer is the "spiritual" world "out there" and the natural world "here." Instead, you have people doing something very much in this world (taking a drug) and experiencing something in that spiritual world so pro-foundly that they change their whole way of viewing both worlds.

This intersection is not something that would have surprised a medieval thinker. The great 13th century theologian Thomas Aquinas argued angels and demons do indeed interact with this world.[57] He viewed these entities as bodiless and comprised of only an intellect and a will. Lacking a corporeal form, an angel could assume an appearance by projecting an image into our minds. This would bring us into the presence of a real entity even if the encounter took place completely within our brains. Putting aside any theology of biblical angels or demons, one could ask: is it possible that DMT does something to our brain chemistry that enables us to come into contact with bodiless beings that can manipulate our minds?

But for many, the language of the spiritual sounds more like fairy tales than real life. So perhaps there is another way to look at these observations in a way that might make more sense to a materialist.

Aquinas wrote so much about angels he has been referred to as the angelic doctor.

As we have seen, we cannot explain away these experiences by looking at brain chemistry. Brain chemistry can at best be described as a mechanism, but it doesn't explain the object of the experience or whether the things seen are simply hallucinations or something real. Furthermore, many of the things seen and felt are very difficult to explain away with "hallucination," and some of the people most likely to do so (atheists) don't, once they have actually taken a psychedelic drug themselves.

So let's consider what it might be that they are seeing, if not a hallucination.

Many have speculated that perhaps hallucinogens allow us to see into a dimension that we would not have otherwise had access to. For example, Michael Pollan writes,

> "Quantum mechanics holds that matter may not be as innocent of mind as the materialist would have us believe. For example, a subatomic particle can exist simultaneously in multiple locations, as pure possibility, until it is measured—that is, perceived by a mind. Only then and not a moment sooner does it drop into reality as we know it: acquire fixed coordinates in time and space. The implication here is that matter might not exist as such in the absence of a perceiving subject. Needless to say, this raises some tricky questions for a materialist understanding of

consciousness. The ground underfoot may be much
less solid than we think."[58]

And he is right that quantum mechanics do muddy our
understanding of reality. But his comments on coordinates
bring the question of dimensions, and it is there that things
get very interesting. For example, in *The Grand Design*,
atheist Stephen Hawking speculates that there may be up
to ten dimensions based on quantum theory.[59] And while
Hawking describes the other dimensions as "small," he does
so with the analogy of looking at the end of a straw — that is,
they only appear small thanks to our perspective, not based
on their actual size.[60] Other scientists such as astrophysicist
Paul Sutter speculate that "dark matter" — a substance
thought to account for more than 80% of the universe's
mass, yet invisible to us — could potentially be explained
by forces and matter being present in other dimensions.[61]
While this research is new and still highly speculative,
it should at least provide an intellectual foundation for
holding that these other dimensions contain attributes that
are not yet known to us.

The possibility that a fourth — or more —spatial
dimension may contain entities is something that has

[58] Pollan, 41.
[59] "There will be a quantum probability amplitude for every number of large
space dimensions from zero to ten." Hawking, 2010, 141.
[60] Hawking, 2010, 141.
[61] Sutter, 2021.

long been speculated. Could this hidden dimension be the source of entities observed while in the ecstatic states, both drug and naturally induced, that we discussed in Chapter 3?

Anthropologist W.Y. Evans-Wenz notes in his *Fairy Faith in Celtic Countries,*

> *"It is mathematically possible to conceive fourth-dimensional beings, and if they exist it would be impossible in a third-dimensional plane to see them as they really are. Hence the ordinary apparition is non-real as a form, whereas the beings, which wholly sane and reliable seers claim to see when exercising seership of the highest kind, may be as real to themselves and to the seers as human beings are to us here in the third-dimensional world when we exercise normal vision."[62]*

Researcher David Luke argues that the geometry often seen while consuming DMT might also point to another dimension. He writes,

> *"[Evans-Wenz's] perception has some resonance with my own observations about the frequently extra-dimensional nature of DMT geometry. [Andrew] Gallimore's perverse metatechnological ontology of the Simulated Universe Theory similarly demands that any artificially intelligent simulated universe,*

---

[62] Luke, DMT Dialogues, 2018, 301.

such as our own, must be created by higher-order technologists existing in a world with more dimensions than this one."[63]

Similarly, in his book *Supernatural,* Graham Hancock speculates that there might be entities within these other dimensions.

"*We might feel very sure that there is no more to reality than the material world in which we live, but we cannot prove that this is the case. Theoretically, there could be other realms, other dimensions, as all religious traditions and quantum physics alike maintain. Theoretically, the brain could be as much a receiver as a generator of consciousness and thus might be fine-tuned in altered states to pick up wavelengths that are normally not accessible to us.*"[64]

Of course, Evans-Wenz, Luke, and Hancock are not coming to these conclusions as theoretical physicists might. They are coming at it as laymen reflecting on research and their experiential backgrounds. But it is interesting to consider that there might be room for overlap in ideas between the ancient religions and modern science. Perhaps the ancients discovered something that modern science

---

[63] Luke, DMT Dialogues, 2018, 301.
[64] Hancock, Visionary: The Mysterious Origins of Human Consciousness (The Definitive Edition of Supernatural), 2022, 30.

is just starting to scratch? Later in *Supernatural* Hancock speculates exactly this,

> *"It may be that DMT makes us able to perceive what the physicists call 'dark matter' …that at present remains invisible to our senses and instruments."*[65]

When I read Hancock's speculation on this point, I was immediately struck by the idea because my training in Christian theology also spoke of other dimensions.

When most people think of Christianity's heaven, they think of a place and time. Heaven is a place you go when you die, but few have formed hard opinions on what it actually is. Some imagine a cloud somewhere. Some imagine a state of mind. But Oxford New Testament scholar N.T. Wright argues that the biblical understanding of heaven must also be described in terms of "dimension." In *Surprised by Hope*, Wright writes, "Heaven in the Bible is not a future destiny but the other hidden dimension of our ordinary life — God's dimension, if you like."[66] And so we have an interesting overlap between traditional Christianity, ancient paganism, cutting-edge astrophysics, and the experiences that take place when someone is on psychedelics. If confirmation of an idea grows as more sources of knowledge confirm it, it

---

[65] Hancock, Visionary: The Mysterious Origins of Human Consciousness (The Definitive Edition of Supernatural), 2022, 386.
[66] Wright, 2008, 19.

seems that the idea that other dimensions exist, and that some interaction with them takes place in this world, is an idea that is gathering a firm foundation.

What if there is some sort of spiritual or heavenly dimension that overlaps and coexists with our own? What if something in our brains prevents us from seeing into it? What if changing our brain chemistry, like clearing blocked ears, allows us to see what we normally do not? In *DMT: The Spirit Molecule,* Strassman argues that DMT can be naturally released by the pineal gland, and that this is part of the basis of a soul's movement in and out of the body; DMT released by the pineal gland as part of what leads to things like heightened states of consciousness. These effects are seen naturally during meditation, sex, prayer, near-death experiences, etc. Strassman states, "DMT could trigger a period of remarkable progress in the scientific exploration of the most mystical regions of the human mind and soul." [67]

As we speculated, what if psychedelics give us vision to see that which we are usually blind to — vision into another dimension? This has been described as the 'ecstatic vision' by mystics, and N.T. Wright would describe it as the "heavenly dimension." But whatever we call it, what if it is real and there are real entities there?

[67] Strassman R. , DMT: The Spirit Molecule: A Doctor's Revolutionary Research Into the Biology of Near-Death and Mystical Experiences, 2000.

What if the beings within that dimension can see into our dimensions, but we cannot see into theirs? Consider Hawking's straw analogy. Imagine a thin diameter straw. If you are positioned at the end of the straw it appears almost invisible— a small dot. But if you are positioned at the side of the straw the whole object becomes visible.

Imagine our own dimension being situated such that we cannot see into the heavenly dimension, but that the beings in that dimension are able to step into ours and then back into their own. If true, this would be shocking. It would force us to wonder if the myths of old were really fiction. What if the apparitions of gods, spirits, demons, and angels were not always or necessarily based on pure human imagination? What if some of them represent true interactions between humans who live in the four visible dimensions (height, width, depth, and time) with entities that live in some other dimension (the heavenly one)? What if the stories of old are, in part, accounts of people being able to see into the other dimension via drugs, meditation, prayer, music, etc.?

An answer in the affirmative would provide much explanatory power in human history. It would explain why so many people in so many places have experienced such similar things. It would explain why people seem to gain genuine insights about things they should not otherwise know. It would explain why almost all human civilizations have been so religious. It would explain why we all seem to have this built-in idea of a soul. It might explain why consciousness exists. It might give insight into why we all love music so much. As physicists speculate on other dimensions to explain dark matter and the workings of the universe, we can also explain quite a bit about the human experience using other dimensions.

So perhaps this is where atheism and religion cease to be separate things. Perhaps all this time we have simply been using different terms. Perhaps atheists use words like *aliens* and *inter-dimensional beings, dark matter,* and *alternative dimensions,* while the religious use words like *gods, angels, demons, spirits,* and *heaven?* Atheists might find it helpful to view these new discoveries as similar to when we found new species in new frontiers — something like when we first went into the depths of the ocean floor and discovered otherworldly-looking sea creatures that resembled monsters from myths. Perhaps atheists need to put the mystical visions in this category. What if the visions represent a discovery of some new frontier that has heretofore been invisible to us?

But for the religious, the ability to see into this heavenly dimension is not as new. So let us now look at some of the ways that religions have historically viewed spiritual entities, and consider how that might impact and interact with what we have learned so far.

V
Mythology in the Real World

When I was a child, I was given a book about the Norse gods. It was beautifully illustrated and told, through graphics and text, the many stories of Thor, Loki, Oden, and all their adventures in the halls of Valhalla. I remember lying in my room and enjoying the tales of trickery, treachery, heroism, and adventure as I flipped through the pages. As I got older, I learned of the parallels between the Norse gods and the gods of the Greeks, Romans, Egyptians, and other pagan religions. These religious ideas seemed completely different from the majority religion around me — Christianity.

The main difference seemed very simple: Christians had one God who was philosophical and reasonable. Pagans had many gods, who tended to be erratic and flawed.

Polytheism and monotheism. One God versus many gods. And I think that is how most people view the differences. But the reality is a bit more complicated. When we read the great pagan philosophers of Greece and Rome, we find that *they too* had a form of monotheism.

Aristotle spoke of a philosophical "Heaven" or "Divine." Using the principles of logic, he argued that the universe required an unmoved mover — a first cause. This cause he described as the "Divine." This Divine, he argued, had to be omnipresent, omniscient, omnipotent, and immutable. This "God of the philosophers" was fundamentally different from the gods we think of when we talk about ancient Norse, Roman, or Greek gods.[68]

Stanley Sfekas, a Professor of Philosophy and Religion at the University of Indianapolis, writes,

> *"Aristotle conceived of God as outside of the world, as the final cause of all motion in Nature, as Prime Mover and Unmoved Mover of the universe. He was the crowning objective of all dynamic development in the cosmos from matter to form and from potentiality to actuality. He stood outside the Great Chain of Being yet was the source of all motion and development."*[69]

Scholars debate whether Aristotle believed in the traditional Greek gods (it appears he was skeptical of some of the stories).[70] I take the view that he was at least open to their

---

[68] Aristotle, De Caelo, I.9, 279 a17–30.
[69] Sfekas.
[70] MorSegev, Aristotle on Religion, Cambridge University Press, 2017, 192.

existence. But regardless of Aristotle's personal views, many who followed him maintained both the concept of the Divine and the concept of lesser gods. As Mor Segev, Professor of Philosophy at the University of South Florida, writes, many Stoics embraced both. "It is salutary in this regard to read the Stoic Cleanthes' 'Hymn to Zeus' to see the possibility of a non-ironic, sincere embrace of the affective side of traditional religion along with [philosophically oriented conceptions]."[71]

Early Christians were struck by how similar the speculations about God by Aristotle and other Greek philosophers were to Christian theology. Biblical theology states that there is one Creator God who is God of all and overall. From him, the Bible tells us, all things are made. He is present everywhere. He is unchanging. He is all-powerful. In short, the biblical God is omnipresent, omniscient, omnipotent, and immutable. He is a God not unlike that described by Aristotle.

But contrary to popular opinion, Christianity does not completely reject the lower gods of paganism; there is a place for lower god-like beings within the Bible. The Old Testament at times sounds like it is polytheistic. It speaks of the God of Israel as "God of gods" (Joshua 22:22). It speaks of him judging other gods (Psalm 82:1). It speaks of him being "above other gods" (Psalm 135:5).

------

[71] MorSegev, Aristotle on Religion, Cambridge University Press, 2017, 192.

So is the Bible polytheistic? No. The picture painted in the Bible and in the writings of the early Christians is that the gods of the pagans exist but represent spirits and demons, not the "true God" or the omnipresent "Creator God." They are subordinate and subject to Israel's God.

This is stated most explicitly in St. Paul's first letter to the Corinthians,

> *"Do I mean then that a sacrifice offered to an idol is anything, or that an idol is anything? No, but the sacrifices of pagans are offered to demons, not to God, and I do not want you to be participants with demons." (1 Corinthians 10:19-20)*

So if we were to sketch the theology of the Greek philosophers, we might get this:

The God of the Philosophers

The Pantheon of Gods: Zeus, Dionysus, etc.

Humans

And if we sketch the theology of the Bible we get this:

Some other ancient religions (e.g., elements of Hinduism and Zoroastrianism) have parallels to this three-tiered theology, but more common in the ancient world was simple polytheism — divorced from Greek philosophy or the Hebrew conception of the Creator God—where the top level is absent and the pantheon of gods are worshiped as the highest beings.

In the Old Testament, we see Israel interacting with other nations (Hittites, Canaanites, Amorites, Phoenicians, Egyptians, etc.), and almost without exception, those nations worship these second-tier types of gods. These gods are provincial, mercurial, and limited in power. But the Bible never says they are non-existent. Instead, they are viewed as (at least potentially) real beings that God can either rule over or crush at will. There is a fundamental difference between the God of Israel and these other gods; the same word is used, but fundamentally the two species are not remotely the same.

This is perhaps why the ancient Hebrews and early Christians were so particular about the form of worship of their God. Images of their God were banned (Exodus 20:2). Worship of any other god was prohibited (Exodus 23:24). When people bow down to angels in scripture, they make it clear that nothing other than the Creator God (not even angels) is worthy of worship (Revelation 22:8-9). This was a High God. A Divine. This was not in the same category. He was a God that could not be seen. He was a God that came before all things. He ordained all things. He knew all things. He was everywhere. He was unchanging.

On the other hand, second-tier entities (described as gods, demons, and angels), while powerful, lacked most of those qualities. They were imperfect. They were prone to wicked pranks and machinations. Finite in size. Able to appear and disappear, yet also able to be seen. They were immortal, yet had a beginning.

Now here is the funny thing. When it comes to this tiered theology, the top-level "Divine" seems much more reasonable and realistic. A benevolent and all-powerful

God that is guiding the world is something that first-class intellectuals throughout the ages have been able to understand and largely agree with. But the pagan deities, with their trickery, shifty behavior, and great but limited power, seem intellectually implausible. As reviewed above, even Aristotle expressed doubts. And in today's world, the second-tier deities are a joke. The idea of sincerely believing in the Greek Zeus or the Aztec Quetzalcoatl seems like something no modern person could do. And yet—

Interestingly, it is this second-tier full of flawed, tricky, and sometimes cruel gods in whom belief is far more universally held. Almost every sociological group in history (including, as we have seen, Christianity) has believed this second tier to be real beings. How is it that the beings that seem the least plausible are the ones that are far more universally adhered to?

Considering what we reviewed in Chapters 3 and 4, is it possible that the reason these gods are so universally accepted is that they are somehow based on real observations? Is it possible that these are not imaginary beings made up out of whole cloth? What if these "gods" are real beings who live (mostly) in another dimension? What if throughout the ages and across cultures, these beings have been encountered, spoken with, and then worshiped? One might even wonder if modern-day visions of aliens (both sober encounters and the aliens seen while on DMT) are in this category?

If so, this would explain a lot. It would explain the universal nature of these beliefs. It would also explain why there are striking parallels across seemingly disconnected cultures as to the nature of the gods — who they are, what they look like, and what they want — and that will be the subject of Chapter 6. But first, we must ask how, if people across cultures and times are all seeing this second tier of gods, they are doing so? And if our argument thus far is sound, hallucinogenic drugs have to be at least one potential explanation.

How common were hallucinogenic drugs in the religions of the ancient world? The answer is that the use of drugs for spiritual purposes was quite common in the ancient world. Many have the impression that the counter-culture of the 1960s somehow discovered drugs, but the use of hallucinogenic drugs for ritual, magical, or spiritual purposes is as old as time. As Graham Hancock said, *"Shamanism is not confined to specific socio-economic settings or stages of development."*[72]

On every continent, throughout all of history, the practice is found. There are many good reasons to believe that the Greeks used hallucinogens (even if their practices

---

[72] Hancock G. , Visionary: The Mysterious Origins of Human Consciousness (The Definitive Edition of Supernatural), 2022, 451.

were kept secret).[73,74,75]The s hamanic u se o f d rugs i s e ven
more clearly seen further north on the European continent,
in the Gaelic and Danish traditions. The Vikings famously
employed an LSD-like drug before going on raiding parties.
And evidence of various hallucinogens being used among
the Germanic tribes (sometimes mixed with wine) is well
documented forensically.[76]

There is very good evidence that various hallucinogens
were used for religious purposes in Ancient Egypt.[77]For
example, the blue water lily (an indication of DMT-based
hallucinogens) has been found in Egyptian jars. As Graham
Hancock notes, there is "No question that psychedelics
were used."[78] We know that many nations in the Ancient
Near East, like the Philistines, likely used psychedelics to
meet the gods. [79]And we know that the various nations and
tribes of Mesoamerica used them.[80]

We will review these practices in more depth in the
next chapter and beyond, but when we talk about the use

---

[73] Muraresku 25.
[74] Broad, 2002.
[75] Muraresku, 26.
[76] Muraresku, 123-126.
[77] Coulter-Harris, 2016, 77.
[78] Graham Hancock on Joe Rogan Podcast #1543
[79] Interestingly, Nineveh at times ruled over the Philistines who were known
for using LSD like drugs. Austin, 2015.
[80] Prince, 2019.

of drugs for spiritual and mystical experiences, we are not talking about a new technology but a very old one. And to return to the main subject of this chapter, if people were seeing real entities when they spoke of the gods, we must consider the possibility that these entities were at least at times being observed through the use of drugs.

In our next chapter, we will discuss who these entities were, and what they asked from the people who encountered them. We will also discuss one very interesting theme that occurs across many religious traditions: the theme of the serpent.[81]

[81] Wilson, 2001.

VI
The Serpent and the Sacrifice

I live a few hours' drive from Serpent Mound in Ohio. This beautiful pre-Columbian earthwork is so big (1,348 feet long) that it can only be seen properly from the sky. It sits on a plateau along the Ohio Brush Creek near Columbus. The mouth of the giant serpent points to the summer solstice sunset, so that when the sun goes down that day it appears that the serpent is swallowing it. The curves of the serpent's body point to other celestial events, including the winter solstice and the equinox.

Precisely who created this magnificent beast, and why, we do not know. Archeologists even debate its age. It is just a giant ancient beautiful serpent pointing to the skies. But one thing is known: whatever tribe or nation built the mound, its creators were not the only ancients to consider serpents central to their religion and their identity.

In the book of Genesis, after God created everything, he put Adam and Eve in a garden and warned them not to eat from a particular tree. A serpent appeared to the woman.

The serpent said, *"Hath God said, Ye shall not eat of every tree of the garden?"* And the woman explained God's prohibition and warning to the serpent. But the serpent dismissed this, "Ye s*hall not surely die,"* and argued that God was prohibiting the fruit of the tree out of fear that they would acquire knowledge that would make them like God. He said, *"For God doth know that in the day ye eat thereof, then your eyes shall be opened, and ye shall be as gods, knowing good and evil."*

The woman considered the words of the serpent, looked at the fruit of the tree, and desired not only to eat of it but to get the knowledge it offered. And so she took it and ate it, and then gave it to the man. Then Genesis tells us, *"The eyes of them both were opened."*And those that know their Bible will realize that it is at this moment that a fundamental break happened between the Divine and the human race. As in the story of Pandora, a box had been opened and hardship came upon the human race. All the pains, sorrows, and struggles of this life —including death itself — are said to have come from this decision.

After pronouncing the curse that resulted, God turned to the serpent and cursed the serpent. And he stated that from that point forward there would be an ongoing battle between the serpent and the human race. *"I will put enmity between thee and the woman, and between thy seed and her seed; it shall bruise thy head, and thou shalt bruise his heel."*

Atheists laugh at this story. They laugh at how Christians around the world could possibly believe in a talking serpent. They wonder why God might be so upset about them eating a plant. They wonder how doing so could possibly bring so much hardship into the world.

But what if there is more to this story than meets the eye?

The Serpent and the Fruit

An interesting observation in the study of psychedelics is that encounters with a serpent are a common experience—especially among those who take ayahuasca and DMT.[82] But other forms of hallucinogens also produce the same vision. As I prepared to write this book, I read countless first-hand accounts of psychedelic experiences from people who had taken LSD, psilocybin, and mescaline, and the serpent was a prevalent vision. A study posted by the University of Chicago Press stated that "visions of demons or snakes" are one of the "consistent" trips while on LSD.[83]

---

[82] Pascal, Luke, & Robinson, 2021.
[83] Dyck, 2020.

The vision is so common that scientists have tried to explain it. For example, anthropologist Jeremy Narby's work on DMT links the pervasion of snake symbolism to our genetic code's molecular structure— it's so common that he ties it to "the internal coding of life itself."[84]

It is important to note that serpents are not the only entities seen while on DMT or other hallucinogens. Many other animals, humanoids, and human-animal hybrids are also common. Further, it is important to note that not everyone who takes psychedelics sees entities at all. In my own psychedelic experience, I experienced strange lights, profound thoughts, and many otherworldly sensations (all very spiritual) but not entities. Yet the vision of serpents is quite common and is worth looking at for this reason.

It appears that people around the world have been interacting with some sort of serpent entity since the dawn of civilization. As we will see in this chapter, the serpent is incredibly common in ancient literature and myths around the world. Also, if we are going to study what effects psychedelic-induced entities might have on people and societies, this is one interaction where we have an abundance of data(both in the ancient and modern worlds).

Graham Hancock states that he has interacted with the serpent entity many times. He refers to the serpents as "the

---

[84] Attala, 2011.

ancient teachers of mankind." He writes of his experiences taking ayahuasca, saying,

> "Very commonly these entities appear as serpents or as serpent human hybrids. Mother Ayahuasca herself...is frequently depicted as a serpent... I have met her in this form many times."

Those raised reading medieval stories of dragons may have a slight uneasy feeling as they hear Hancock's happy discussion of encountering a woman who also appears as a serpent; serpents and dragons are the prototypical villains in medieval Christian folklore. In addition to writing children's books, C.S. Lewis was a professor of medieval literature at Oxford. In *The Silver Chair*, Lewis makes the principal antagonist a woman that turns into a serpent. Lewis, who was steeped in stories of the Middle Ages, certainly pulled this theme from that folklore. And in another work from the Chronicles of Narnia, *The Voyage of the Dawn Treader*, Lewis discusses the danger of not knowing about giant serpents, "Most of us know what we should expect to find in a dragon's lair, but...Eustace had read only the wrong books...they were weak on dragons." And perhaps the same could be said for Hancock.

Why were dragons such hated figures in European history?[85] Perhaps, with Europe's strong Christian

---

[85] It is worth noting that stories of dragon slaying are not only found in Christian

traditions, people got the character of the evil serpent from the Bible itself. The Bible starts with a serpent as the principal antagonist, but it certainly does not stop there. Those opening verses foreshadow an ongoing struggle between the serpent and humanity throughout the biblical canon.

Starting with the story of Eve, the serpent in the Bible keeps raising its head throughout the pages. For example, in the book of Exodus, Chapter 7, Moses battles the magicians of Egypt. God gives him the ability to control a serpent (that was formed using his staff) in a way that overpowers and destroys the serpents of the Egyptian magicians.

In the book of Numbers, Chapter 21, the serpent is used as a form of medicine. Moses creates serpents of brass that, when held up, heal the plague-stricken Israelites. But then the Bible tells us that the Israelites started to worship the serpents in 2 Kings 18:3-4.[86]

In Psalm 58, we read that the wicked have the venom of the serpent. In Isaiah 27:1, as the prophet is describing the

---

cultures, but in others as well, with perhaps one of the earliest stories dating back to Sumerian lore. See Leslie S. Wilson, *The Serpent Symbol in the Ancient Near East*, 30. But Christendom's recurring legends of dragon slaying are more pronounced and more common than in other cultures.

[86] An interesting question, given the overlap between serpent worship and drug use, about this story from Numbers 21 and 2 Kings 18 is that perhaps part of Moses' cure was not just the bronze serpent but some sort of drug that served as a medicine. Is it possible that the people of Israel took drugs that healed their disease and then became a part of religious worship like so many tribes around them?

redemption of God, he writes, "In that day God shall bring his holy and great and strong sword upon the dragon, even the serpent that flees…he shall destroy the dragon."

In the New Testament, Jesus asks what father, if their child is hungry will give him a serpent rather than food (Matthew 7:10).

And to provide the closing bookend to the Bible, the book of Revelation by St. John states:

> "And I saw an angel come down from heaven, having the key of the bottomless pit and a great chain in his hand. And he laid hold on the dragon, that old serpent, which is the Devil, and Satan, and bound him a thousand years, and cast him into the bottomless pit, and shut him up, and set a seal upon him, that he should deceive the nations no more, till the thousand years should be fulfilled: and after that, he must be loosed a little season." (Revelation 20:1-3)

In this vision of the end of times, St. John says that the serpent will be chained and locked away for many years. But when that serpent gets out, John says, he will be loosed again to deceive and destroy.[87]

So the image of the serpent as the enemy of mankind is found throughout the Bible, but for Christendom, it

---

[87] The phrase "a thousand years" in the Bible is thought to not be an exact number so much as a phrase that meant, "a long time."

certainly does not stop there. The theme of fighting against serpents and dragons is very familiar to anyone familiar with European folklore. Dragon stories are as old as storytelling itself.

The third-century Saint Margaret of Antioch, after being tortured for her faith during the Diocletianic Persecution, was thrown back into her cell only to be confronted by a dragon. Fortunately, she thought to make the sign of the cross and the dragon vanished.[88]In ancient France, a deadly dragon known as "La Gargouille" was causing floods on the river Seine, and the people of the nearby town of Rouen were forced to offer the dragon a human sacrifice once each year. Thankfully a priest named Romanus promised that, if the people built a church, he would rid them of the dragon. Once the church was built, Romanus followed through on his promise, killed La Gargouille, and mounted his head on the wall. And to this day, that is why France has gargoyles on their church roofs.[89]

Perhaps the most famous of all is the story of Saint George, the patron saint of England. Like in the poor city of Rouen, the people of Saint George's community were being menaced by a dragon that demanded human sacrifice. One day, when the dragon sought to consume the princess, Saint George intervened. He stabbed the beast. Then, like Saint

---

[88] de Voragine, 2012.
[89] Sherman 2015, 183–184.

Margaret, he subdued the dragon with a sign of the cross. The defeated dragon was then led like a dog by Saint George and the princess into the town, and George promised to kill it if the townspeople would convert to Christianity. When the town converted, Saint George followed through on his promise and killed the dragon, and the city was menaced no more. Notice a theme here of dragons destroying and demanding human sacrifice, followed by Christian missionaries defeating and putting down the dragon.

Let us step back and consider where these dragons — these giant, human-sacrifice-demanding serpents — were coming from. As far as we know, there were no giant serpents in this era of human history. But, as we touched on briefly in the previous chapter and we will review in more depth shortly, there was widespread use of drugs for spiritual purposes in ancient Europe. And as discussed above, the observation of serpents while on certain forms of hallucinogens is a very common experience.

And we know of at least one ancient myth where drugs were used for this exact purpose. In Greek mythology, Medea, the daughter of King Aeëtes of Colchis, deployed her drugs to conjure up phantom dragons for the mythical King Pelias.

"By means of certain drugs, Medea caused shapes of Drakonas to appear, which she declared had brought

the goddess through the air from the Hyperborean's to make her stay with Pelias."[90]

Given how common visions of serpents are while on ayahuasca and other psychedelics, and given how common serpents are in ancient mythologies around the world, it seems very plausible that at least some of the myths are based on actual interactions with serpents via the use of drugs as the story of Medea appears to confirm.

Historians have also noticed another common theme: serpent gods and human sacrifice t end t o g o t ogether. The c ombination of t he s erpent g od a nd h uman s acrifice is very well known in the study of the Ancient Near East. As Leslie Wilson, a Research Associate in the Near Eastern Languages Department at Yale University, writes in *The Serpent Symbol in the Ancient Near East*, "We have already admitted the practice of sacrifice of h uman b eings i n the ancient world as a datum." He notes that the serpent and the sacrifice are "inextricably linked."[91] He states that these sacrifices are done at the "ultimate bequest to the gods."[92] So, at least in the Ancient Near East, serpents demanding human sacrifice are "a datum."

If the religious use of drugs was common in this era, *and* the observation of serpent gods while on hallucinogens

---

[90] DiodorusSiculus, Library of History 4. 50. 6 (trans. Oldfather).
[91] Wilson, 2001, 216.
[92] Wilson, 2001, 24.

was common, *and* the demand of serpent gods for human sacrifice was common, we can connect all three "datums" and see a significant parallel to the dragon stories of ancient Christendom — dragons demanding human sacrifice only to be driven out and killed by Christian missionaries. And when we look at the history and practices of the religions that Christian missionaries would have encountered as Christianity expanded, this parallel becomes harder to avoid. Let us survey the world the missionaries met.

The Bible's Old Testament was born out of the historic region of Western Asia situated within the Tigris–Euphrates river system known to us today as Mesopotamia. The Hebrew people that wrote the Old Testament spoke of various other groups including the Canaanites, Amorites, the Philistines, and others inhabiting the region we now know as Israel. The region had many gods including Asherah. Asherah was depicted either as a serpent or the bride of a serpent.[93] Also in the region of the Hebrews were the Phoenicians, who worshipped an undying serpent they called the "Good Demon."[94] The ancient biblical writers had interactions with the people of Cyprus, who also worshipped a serpent deity who required human sacrifice, there were many other serpent deities in this region as well. [95] [96]

---

[93] Wilson, 103.

[94] Wilson, 2001, 62. Note that the Good Demon (the agathosdaimon) was also worshiped in Egypt.

[95] Wilson, 2001, 27.

[96] Tolentino, 2022.

Many Mesopotamian peoples who worshipped these gods used drugs for spiritual purposes (more on this in the next chapter).[97]And as we see in Wilson's survey, human sacrifice was common throughout the region. It was so common that the Bible makes repeated warnings against the temptation to sacrifice children in the fire.[98,99]

In Egypt, human sacrifice was not common in most eras, but there were periods—notably around 2,500 B.C. — in Lower Egypt in which human sacrifice became "systematic and substantial".[100] Interestingly, in this same period and region, Egyptians had started to worship a serpent god named Wadjet.[101]And as we have already seen, there is very good evidence that the Egyptians also used drugs during their religious practices. So, in the region that birthed the Bible, there are clear indications of the ritual use of drugs, serpent gods, and human sacrifice. [102]

Drugs for spiritual purposes, serpent gods, and human sacrifice.

In the Hellenistic world of the New Testament, there were similar cultural themes. Greek mythology is full of serpents. We see the staff of Hermes (Caduceus), the dragon of Triptolemus, and sanctuaries built on high hills in Greece

---

[97] See a more extended discussion on the Septuagint see Chapter 7.
[98] e.g Deuteronomy 12:31.
[99] e.g. 2 Kings 16:3.
[100] Recht, 2020.
[101] Hill.
[102] Warmington, 441–464.

that, "teemed with the imagery of snakes, sea monsters and serpent tailed human composite figures," according to Joan Breton Connelly, a classical archaeologist at New York University.[103] Serpents were so prevalent in the worship of the Greeks that a real snake was kept on the Acropolis to guard the Sacred Rock.[104]

The cult of Dionysus is thought to have secretly employed psychedelics; this cult, interestingly, was also rich with serpentine symbolism.[105] Additionally, many speculate that evidence of rituals found at Delphi and Eleusis involved the use of hallucinogens.[106] There is controversy about whether the Greeks practiced human sacrifice; it is spoken of in their poems and histories, but scholars debate the extent to which it really took place.[107,108] We do know, however, that the ancient Greeks were not averse to the shedding of innocent blood, as infanticide was widely practiced.[109]

Drugs for spiritual purposes, serpent gods, and slaughter of innocents.

As Christianity grew and Christians moved further north, they would have found similar themes. Many people

---

[103] Connelly, 46.

[104] Connelly, 46.

[105] Wilson, 2001, 38.

[106] For Delphi, see National Geographic Staff, 2001. And for Eleusis see Muraresku, 2020, 83-105.

[107] Daley, 2016.

[108] Wilson, 2001, 28-29.

[109] Pomeroy, 1983, 207-222.

know that Saint Patrick (born 385 AD) is said to have banished the snakes from Ireland, but few know that he is also said to have banished all demons. The antiquarian John O'Donovan (1806-1861) tells us that the demons (perhaps led by the Celtic god Crum Dubh) were believed to have been overcome when Saint Patrick threw his black bell at them. He battled them on the high mountaintop where Crum Dubh lived. Then Cora, the snake goddess, who was thought to be Crum Dubh's mother, fell to Patrick at Loch Nacorra.[110]

As the medieval Monk Jocelyn of Scotland wrote,

> *"Ireland since its first habitation had been pestered with a triple plague, namely, a great abundance of venomous reptiles, with myriads of demons visibly appearing, and with a multitude of magicians…The glorious apostle labored by prayer and other exercises of devotion to deliver the island from triple pestilence. Taking the Staff of Jesus in his hand he hurled the reptiles into Lognan Deamhan."[111]*

Archeologists and Celtic scholars are convinced that Ireland never had snakes — whatever serpents were there were not the sort of snakes we meet in rivers and fields. So scholars speculate that perhaps Saint Patrick did not literally

---

[110] Claffey, 2016.
[111] Claffey, 2016.

exterminate the snakes, but that the story represents the way Christianity put down the serpent-filled religions of the Celts and the Druids.[112]

The Celts also used hallucinogens in their worship.[113] Authors Erynn Rowan Laurie and Timothy White write, "[The] abundance of Celtic legends about crimson foods which induce mystical experiences, inspire extraordinary knowledge, and impart the gift of prophecy, is highly suggestive."[114,115] Their contention echoes ethnomycologist R. Gordon Wasson and others who made the compelling case for the widespread use of the psychedelic mushroom *Amanita muscaria* in the region of the Celts and Gauls.[116,117,118]

Finally, it is well established that the Druids practiced human sacrifice. Julius Caesar was among the first to report on this in his writings about his escapades through northern Europe; he famously wrote that the native Celts, "believe that the gods delight in the slaughter of prisoners and criminals, and when the supply of captives runs short, they sacrifice even the innocent." Elsewhere he wrote that in times of danger, the Celts believed that "unless the life

[112] Claffey, 2016.
[113] ed. John A Rush, 2013, 307.
[114] Laurie & White., 1997.
[115] Laurie & White, 1997.
[116] Wasson, 1967.
[117] Saar, 1991.
[118] Wilson, P. L., 1999, 15.

of a man be offered, the mind of immortal gods will not favor them." Roman author Pliny the Elder (born 23 AD) stated that the Celts practiced ritual cannibalism, eating their enemies' flesh as a source of spiritual and physical strength.[119]

And we have archeological evidence to back up these claims. In the 1980s, a 2,000-year-old, bog-mummified body was discovered. A young man's head had been violently smashed, he had been strangled, and his throat was slashed. Then his neck had been constricted with a rope near the cut to "cause an enormous fountain of blood to rise up."[120]

As we draw together these themes, we see that the ancient Celts took drugs for spiritual purposes, worshiped serpent gods, and practiced human sacrifice. And, as in the story of Saint George and Romanus, the dragon was put down by the coming of a Christian saint who drove them out and saved the people from the voracious human-consuming dragon.

The pre-Christian Vikings used a plant called "stinking henbane" as a hallucinogen.[121] Their pantheon included a variety of serpent gods including the Midgard Jormungandr.[122] And they practiced human sacrifice.

---

[119] Owen, 2009.
[120] Owen, 2009.
[121] Blakely, 2020.
[122] Tolentino, 2022.

Bishop Thietmar of Merseburg (born 975 AD), describes how the Vikings met every nine years to "offer to their gods 99 people and just as many horses, dogs and hens or hawks, for these should serve them in the kingdom of the dead and atone for their evil deeds."[123] The monk, Adam of Bremen, wrote a similar account in 1072 A.D. regarding a region of Sweden. In a temple devoted to Thor, Odin, and Frey, the Vikings also met every nine years to sacrifice humans and all kinds of living creatures.[124] There was a time when these accounts were thought to be exaggerations, but recent archaeological finds show that human sacrifice was a reality in the Viking era.[125]

Historian Tom Holland tells an interesting story about how Iceland converted to Christianity. The Icelandic people were feeling increasing pressure to convert so that they could have better trade and military alliances with the rest of Europe. He writes that Thorgeir Thorkelsson, a well-respected pagan priest and leader among the Icelandic people, proclaimed that Iceland should convert to Christianity and that he would himself. But there were three provisions he insisted upon.

First, they could continue to eat horse meat — so far so good. But the second and third provisions show the extent

---

[123] Nationalmuseet i København Staff.
[124] Nationalmuseet i København Staff.
[125] Nationalmuseet i København Staff.

to which the murder of innocents was part of Icelandic culture. Thorkelsson's second provision was that infanticide should be allowed to continue for unwanted babies. And his third was that sacrifice might be allowed to continue on private estates (simply kept out of the public). Knowing what we know from Bishop Thietmar and Monk Adam, there is good reason to suspect these sacrifices included humans.[126]

Once again we encounter the dark trinity of drugs for spiritual purposes, serpent gods, and human sacrifice.

In ancient Mesoamerica, the Maya built beautiful buildings, henges to track the stars, and an amazing empire. They also used various drugs, including mushrooms, to talk to the gods — one of whom was Kukulkan, a feathered serpent god.[127,128] Sadly, the Maya also enslaved millions, engaged in constant war, and drowned little children in sinkholes to appease their gods.

Maya priests in the Yucatan peninsula would convince the gods to make it rain by throwing children as young as three years old into sacred sinkhole caves thought to be the entrance to the underworld. In one grisly find, Archeologist Guillermo de Anda of the University of Yucatan pieced together the bones of 127 boys between the ages of three

---

[126] Holland, 2009, 179-187.
[127] Evans, 2013.
[128] Tigg, 2013.

and eleven that he found at the bottom of one of the nearby sacred caves.[129]

Drugs for spiritual purposes, serpent gods, and human sacrifice.

The Aztecs worshipped Quetzalcoatl, whose name means "precious serpent" and who is described as "The Feathered Serpent, [...who] came to teach [the ancient inhabitants of Mexico] the benefits of settled agriculture and the skills necessary to build temples"[130]

From Quetzalcoatl and other gods, they learned all sorts of great things about healing, astronomy, and technology. And their shamans used mushrooms and other hallucinogens to experience the spirit world.[131] Like the Maya, the Aztecs also engaged in widespread slavery, widespread oppression, and war.

And they practiced human sacrifice.

The rates at which they murdered are legendary. Some scholars put the number of people sacrificed by the Aztecs as high as 250,000 per year![132] The carnage was so great that Spanish conquistador Herman Cortez — a man who had seen plenty of death in his life — was horrified and shocked by the sheer volume of the carnage. Another

[129] Reuters, 2008.
[130] Hancock G. , 2016, 31.
[131] Kristinsson & al, 2009, 122.
[132] Salem Media, 2022.

conquistador, Andrés de Tapia, described the way the sacrifices helped build the Aztec empire. He said that the Aztecs had two rounded towers flanking the Templo Mayor made entirely of human skulls. Between them, he wrote, a towering wooden rack displayed thousands more skulls impaled on wooden poles.[133] The architecture of the Aztecs was literally built with human sacrifice.[134]

Drugs for spiritual purposes, serpent gods, and human sacrifice.

The Inca Empire worshiped various gods including Pachamama. Pachamama was a fertility goddess who watched over planting and harvesting. And this god of the plants was depicted as a woman who sometimes became a dragon.[135] The Inca used ayahuasca to meet Pachamama and the other gods. They learned about the stars. They were given guidance on establishing a powerful empire. And the architectural skills they learned in building — constructing beautiful temples with incredibly precise stonework, using giant stones that they somehow got up into the high mountains — continue to confound even modern scholars. They also tracked the movement of the stars with astonishing precision.

But these worshipers of the dragon and consumers of ayahuasca also enslaved millions. They practiced infanticide. They also practiced constant war.

---

[133] Roos, 2018.
[134] Dwyer & Stout, 2012, 12.
[135] Fenolio & Crump, 2015, 75.

And they sacrificed thousands of children to their gods.

Physical anthropologist John Verano of Tulane University expressed shock when he discovered the remains at one archeological site. What was so jarring to him was the grisly find that he and several other anthropologists uncovered — the skeletal remains of more than 140 children who had been ritually sacrificed on a high a wind-swept bluff overlooking the Pacific Ocean.[136] This find confirmed the many horrific accounts of Inca priests sacrificing countless innocents which Spanish explorers had recorded in their journals.

Drugs for spiritual purposes, serpent gods, and human sacrifice.

What about the North American indigenous peoples? As we saw with Serpent Mound, there were certainly various serpent deities. We also know that the shamans of these tribes made regular use of various hallucinogenic herbs, mushrooms, cacti, and other substances to meet the gods.[137]

Another remarkable mound within a few hours' drive from my house is called Monk's Mound. It was built by the Mississippian culture in what is today Illinois, and is a giant mound of earth that looks amazingly like a dirt version of the Mayan and Aztec pyramids.

---

[136] Romey, 2018.
[137] El-Seedi HR, 2005.

As archeologists have explored the mound, they have made some unpleasant discoveries. Many bones of sacrificed humans have been found. In one gruesome discovery, the bones of 52 young women were found and are thought to have been sacrificed at the same time. In another find, 39 men and women were ritually beaten to death.[138]

Drugs for spiritual purposes, serpent gods, and human sacrifice.

Asia and the east have similar historic themes. Hinduism has serpent worship (e.g., the Five Nagas),[139]and also used an unknown drug called "soma" for spiritual purposes. The Ancient Hindus also practiced *sati* (the burning of a widow with her husband).[140] And human sacrifice was definitely carried out (although to what extent is debated).[141] At a minimum, human sacrifice is listed in the Vedas as the highest of all sacrifices, and there is archeological evidence to show that it was indeed practiced.[142] The same themes are found in China: the shamanic use of drugs.[143]The presence of serpent deities.[144]And human sacrifice.[145]

---

[138] Jarus, 2017.
[139] Tolentino, 2022.
[140] Narasimhan, 1992.
[141] Brighenti, 2005.
[142] Doniger, 2014, 217.
[143] Grinspoon, 1979, 39.
[144] Religion and Society in T'ang and Sung China, 1993, 101.
[145] Religion and Society in T'ang and Sung China, 1993, 301n.

Where history is known, the themes of shamanic drugs, dragons, and human sacrifice are incredibly common. As I noted earlier, we must be careful about not universalizing these things. There are certainly some societies that did not take drugs, did not have serpent gods, and did not practice human sacrifice. But as we explore this question of what the spirits or entities that people encounter while on psychedelics are, the character of the snake casts a shadow throughout the entire ancient world and the demands of this entity appear to be less than beneficent.

So everywhere Christians went, as Christianity spread through the world, it reflected the serpent theme of the Bible. And everywhere it spread, it encountered the spiritual use of drugs and human sacrifice. But thus far, we have not reviewed how Christianity interacted with the central theme of this book: hallucinogens. Let's explore this in the next chapter.

VII
Why Christendom Fights the Dragon

Why has western civilization been so opposed to the religious and spiritual use of drugs? The short answer is Christianity.

It is an interesting thing. As we have seen, religions around the world have regularly used drugs as part of their ceremonies. In fact, for many ancient religions, drugs played a central part. But Christianity is strikingly different. Not only did Christians not use drugs as part of their religion, they also condemned the use of drugs as evil. As Christianity developed from a small sect of Judaism in a corner of the Roman Empire to the largest and most powerful religion in the world, arguably one of the biggest effects was the banishment of the use of drugs for religious purposes.

What was the motivation behind this change from ancient religious norms? Why did Christianity have such an aversion to the practice of using drugs as part of the religious experience? [146]

Some might object that Christianity absolutely *does* command the use of one drug for spiritual purposes: alcohol. And it does so in perhaps the most spiritual practice of all — the Sacrament of the Lord's Supper. Wine is taken every Sunday across the world as part of the Christian Sunday service. But this view is misleading. Christians only take a tiny drink of wine during the sacrament — never enough to alter consciousness — and the Bible explicitly condemns any drunkenness as part of the service.[147]

What about other drugs? What does the Bible say about using drugs like those employed by so many other religions as a way to see the gods? What about learning spiritual insights, as some proponents have suggested? What about healing our minds?

At first glance, in our English translations of the biblical text, we find scant references to drugs. Google "what the Bible says about drugs" and you will find websites pointing

---

[146] Note that the other Abrahamic religions (Islam and Judaism) also share a general aversion to drugs as part of worship. As I argue in this chapter, Christianity likely inherited its aversion from the ancient Jews, and I would further argue that Islam inherited its aversion from Christianity.

[147] "So then, when you come together...one person remains hungry and another gets drunk. Don't you have homes to eat and drink in? ... What shall I say to you? Shall I praise you? Certainly not in this matter!" (1 Corinthians 11:20-22).

to some basic biblical warnings about not getting too drunk from wine. Taken at face value, these would suggest that the Bible has more warnings about wine than it does about ayahuasca or peyote. Perhaps the Rastafarians are right and Christians should sit around smoking ganja in a worshipful way rather than drinking beer at the church picnic. Given this truth, why do most people think of it as so "un-Christian" to sit around having ecstatic visions on ayahuasca?

The answer is that there is something giant missing from the English translations of the Bible. The New Testament was written in an ancient form of Greek called "Koine Greek," and the Old Testament was written in Hebrew. But in the first-century world of Jesus and his Apostles, there was a widely-used Koine Greek translation of the Old Testament called the Septuagint. When the New Testament quotes the Old Testament, it is more often than not the Septuagint that is quoted. So Koine Greek is both the language of the New Testament and the language of the Old Testament Bible that Jesus and his apostles would have read.

And what is the word for "drugs" in Koine Greek? It is "φαρμακεία." Or transliterated to English letters: pharmakeia. If the word "pharmakeia" sounds familiar, it is probably because "pharmakeia" is where we get our English word "pharmacy."

And this word, in its various forms, is found multiple times in the New Testament and throughout the Koine Greek translation of the Old Testament. The reason that it is not translated simply as "drugs" is that the word has another rendering often used by scholars. Because of context, in most biblical instances, scholars translate the various conjugations of *pharmakeia* as one of the following: **witch, wizard, witchcraft, sorcerer, sorcery, divination.**

Yes. The word for *witchcraft* and the word for *drugs* are the same in the language of the Bible.

The Friberg Lexicon defines **pharmakeia** as, "one *who prepares and uses drugs for magical purposes or ritual witchcraft, sorcerer, poisoner, magician.*" The Louw-Nida Lexicon defines it as *"the use of drugs for any kind for magical effect, sorcery, magic."* Liddell-Scott Lexicon defines it as *"the use of drugs, potions, spells..."*[148]

As is clear from these definitions, this is not a case where the same word has two different meanings such as with the English "bark," which can mean either the sound a dog makes or the outer layer of a tree.

No. This is a case where the two translations come out of a single common aspect of sorcery and witchcraft in the ancient world. More often than not, when shamans, witchdoctors, prophetesses, mediums, and sorcerers did

---

[148] Lexicons accessed via BibleWorks software version 6.

their work in the ancient world, a brew of some sort of hallucinogenic form was employed. And the two practices became so associated in the minds of the ancient Greek world that they shared a single word: **pharmakeia**.

As Leslie Wilson notes,

> *"The very uncertainty of the exact lines of demarcation (if any exist) of the boundaries between religion, magic, and medicine, has rendered the theoretical distinctions between them untenable in practice."*[149]

So when the Jews who translated the Hebrew of the Old Testament into Greek to create the Septuagint and the Jewish Apostles who wrote the New Testament used the word **pharmakeia**, they were strongly associating pagan and shamanic rituals and drugs. With this in mind, let's review some of what the Bible says (Old Testament references will be from the Koine Greek of the Septuagint).

Let's start with **Exodus 22:18**. The English translation is:

> *"You shall not allow a sorceress to live."*

The word sorceress is *pharmakous* — a conjugation of pharmakeia — in Koine Greek. The translation using the Friberg Lexicon would be rendered something like this:

---

[149] Wilson, 2001, 69.

"Do not allow one who prepares drugs for ritual purposes to live."

And suddenly what the Bible says about drugs becomes much clearer. The Bible is saying that the mixing of drugs and religion is so bad that the Israelites should not even let someone live who does it!

Let's consider the Greek Septuagint's rendering of **Deuteronomy 18:10**:

"Let no one be found among you who sacrifices his son or daughter in the fire, who practices divination or sorcery, interprets omens, engages in pharmakous."

Notice that statement about human sacrifice. The Bible has several links between human sacrifice (widely practiced by ancient religions that did use drugs as part of their worship, as we saw in the previous chapter) and pharmakeia.

Now consider **2 Chronicles 33:6**, a verse talking about the evil King Manasseh:

"He sacrificed his sons in the fire in the Valley of Ben Hinnom, practiced sorcery, divination, and witchcraft (epharmakeueto), and consulted mediums and spiritists. He did much evil in the eyes of the LORD, provoking him to anger."

This conjugation, *epharmakeueto*, of pharmakeia is rendered thus by the Liddell Scott Lexicon: "1- to administer a drug or 2- to use enchantments." So King Manasseh became so evil that he sacrificed his children in the fire and started administering drugs (with the implication of spiritual or ritualistic usage).

Consider **2 Kings 9:22**:

> *"When Joram saw Jehu he asked, "Have you come in peace, Jehu?""How can there be peace," Jehu replied, "as long as all the idolatry and pharmaka of your mother Jezebel abound?"*

Jezebel is the notoriously evil queen in the Bible. When Jehu lists her two greatest evils, he says, "idolatry and pharmaka." Jewish people such as Christ's earliest followers St. Peter and St. Paul would have grown up reading that one of the two most evil actions of one of the wickedest people in the Bible's included using drugs for spiritual purposes.

Nahum 3:4 records the prophet stating that the city of Ninevah *"enslaved nations by her prostitution and peoples by her pharmaka."*

Many other references in the Old Testament carry this theme on. In **Exodus 9**, the men who prevent Egypt from listening to the warnings of Moses (ultimately bringing on the plagues) were sorcerers (pharmakous). And in **Micah**

5:12, God promises that when he acts he will act to destroy pharmakeia.

To summarize, the Old Testament (as found in the Koine Greek Septuagint) states that those who practice pharmakeia (the ritual/spiritual/magical use of drugs) are not worthy to live. They are the worst sorts of people who deceive whole nations and lead to human sacrifice and blood lust.

In between the closing of the Old Testament canon and the writing of the New Testament, there were a group of books now described as the Apocrypha. These books are accepted as canonical by Roman Catholics and Eastern Orthodox Christians but not by Protestants or Jews. But whether taken as canonical or not, the books were undeniably influential in the early church, and certainly helped shape Christian thinking about the practice of pharmakeia. Consider the book of Wisdom. **Wisdom 12:4** says God hated the Canaanites because of two things: their "wicked sacrifices" (likely human), and their "pharmakeia." Note yet again the close association that the ancient Hebrews had between human sacrifice and pharmakeia.

Now let us move to the New Testament. Things do not get any rosier for those who practice pharmakeia. The Apostle Paul, in **Galatians 5:19-20,** lists pharmakeia as one of the things that are signs of having a sinful nature, and that those who practice such things "will not enter the kingdom of heaven." The Book of Revelation has several condemnations of pharmakeia, including **Revelation 9:21** where a church is condemned for failing to set aside their pharmakeia. One wonders if this early church hoped to learn about God in the same way modern thinkers do, using some ancient Near East version of ayahuasca. **Revelation 21:8** and **Revelation 22:15** list those who practice pharmakeia as the people who will be cast out of the Kingdom on the Day of Judgment.

Interestingly, **Revelation 18:23** says that "all nations were deceived" by the pharmakeia of Babylon. This echoes **Nahum 3:4** where Nineveh enslaved whole nations by her pharmakeia.

Let us stop our review of the biblical teachings on pharmakeia. The biblical indictment against it seems almost unhinged. Here is a summary of what the Bible says:

> *1- Those who practice pharmakeia are not worthy of life (Exodus 22:18).*

> *2-There is a close association between pharmakeia and human sacrifice (Deuteronomy 18:10, 2 Chronicles 33:6, Wisdom 12:4).*

3- It deceives/enslaves whole nations (Revelation 18:23 and Nahum 3:4).

4- Those who practice it will be cast out of God's presence (Galatians 5:20 and Revelation 22:15).

And the earliest doctors of the church maintained this hostility toward pharmakeia. Ignatius of Antioch (c 110 AD) calls the Lord's Supper the "pharmakeia of immortality" in his *Letter to the Ephesians*, leading some to claim that perhaps the Church did not continue this condemnation — but this is misleading. In fact, Ignatius uses the phrase with the specific purpose of differentiating Christianity from the pagan cults.

In the context of his *Letter to the Ephesians*, chapters 19 and 20, Ignatius is arguing that Christianity is not like paganism. He is saying that pagans use sorcery and spells, but that those have lost their power. He argues that real power is in Jesus Christ the King. It is only after this that he notes that the Eucharist is the true "drug of immortality". He is not saying "we are doing the same thing" he is saying that our drug of immortality is this little drink of wine in which Christians partake of Jesus. In other words, he uses the word of the pagans to *differentiate* Christianity, not to make it the same.

And we can be doubly sure that Ignatius was not endorsing φαρμακεία here because elsewhere Ignatius specifically condemns pharmakeia.[150]

---

[150] See Ungit, Did the Early Church Use Psychedelics?, 2022.

But what about other early church fathers? What do they have to say? Among the writings commonly described as "Apostolic Fathers" (writers of the late first and early second century thought to have close connections to the apostles), there are two other authors who discuss pharmakeia, and both speak of it in very negative tones.

In the *Didache* (c 90AD), the author says Christians must not practice magic and do not practice pharmakeia (2.2). Later, he lists pharmakeia as a "way of death" (5.1). Here, one of the earliest Christian documents outside the New Testament makes it clear that pharmakeia and Christianity are completely incompatible. And in the *Shepherd of Hermes*, Vision 3 (early 2nd century), the author says, "Be not like the sorcerers (pharmakois)."

So here we have three of the earliest Christian writings outside the New Testament (Ignatius, *Didache*, and *Shepherd of Hermes*) all unreservedly condemning pharmakeia. And as the centuries unfolded, this attitude in the Church never softened. We see a clear and consistent succession of bishops and church leaders making it clear that pharmakeia had no place in Christianity.

What is going on here? Why is the practice of utilizing drugs for spiritual purposes (so common in so many other cultures) so harshly condemned by ancient Jews, the New Testament, and the earliest church fathers?

From a secular scientific standpoint, it makes no sense. In Chapter 3, we reviewed the studies and experiences of users of hallucinogens and saw that there is at least some data to suggest quantifiable benefits. Many reading these verses have personally experienced pharmakeia in some form. And almost everyone can agree that the effects of a psychedelic trip are not always bad.

But let us consider what we reviewed in Chapters 3, 4, 5, and 6. What if what we experience while on hallucinogens are not in fact hallucinations? What if the spirits we experience and the entities we see are not imaginary, but in some way reflect actual things which are normally invisible to our own dimension?

Let's look at the question like the ancient Jews who wrote the Bible might have looked at it. They believed in spirits, demons, and angels. When they saw people contacting the spiritual world through the use of drugs, they didn't automatically assume that they were hallucinating. Instead, they asked the question that we asked earlier: who are the entities? The ancient Jews clearly concluded that people who take psychedelic drugs and report spiritual experiences really are experiencing spiritual things.

And as we saw in Chapter 4, this is not just a consideration of ancient Jews. Modern thinkers without Christian or Jewish leanings have speculated on the same thing. Consider the words of ethnobotanist and mystic Terence McKenna:

> *"This has to be taken seriously. In other words, the 'it's only a hallucination' thing—that horseshit is just passé. I mean, reality is only a hallucination for crying out loud, haven't you heard? So that takes care of that—it's only a hallucination. What we've got here, folks, is an intelligent entity of some sort that is frantic to communicate with human beings for some reason."*[151]

Here Terence McKenna, an outspoken advocate for the use of psychedelics, agrees with ancient Jews that something more than simple hallucination is going on when we take drugs for spiritual purposes.

As we saw in Chapter 3, people who take large amounts of ayahuasca (or the synthesized version, DMT) report interacting with entities. When they come down from their highs, they state that they are convinced that what they saw was real — that they really did see these entities (some call them elves, aliens, robots, or spirits). Modern people are prone to simply say, "What a weird brain phenomenon." But given everything we have reviewed so far, isn't it reasonable to ask who the entities are? *Shouldn't we ask?*

---

[151] DMT Entities, DMT Times, 2019.

And as we saw in Chapter 5, the earliest Christians had a strong theology of demons. In modern Western parlance, the phrase "spiritual experience" almost always has positive connotations. But the ancients were more discerning. Upon hearing that you had a spiritual experience, they might ask, "which spirits?" Because they believed that not all spirits are good. And for biblical writers, if the spirits are not from God, they are certainly not good spirits. This means that from a biblical perspective there are *bad* spirits. Demons. And, the writers might ask, if we are getting spiritual experiences using a method that God strongly condemns (pharmakeia), what sort of spirits are we interacting with?

Many people dismiss the idea that the spiritual experiences people have while on DMT or other hallucinogens are demonic because the entities often seem good and nice. Further, as we saw in Chapters 2 and 3, the experiences also often have positive effects. Shouldn't this cause us to dismiss any idea that the spirits have any malice or ill intent?

The biblical writers would answer these questions with an unqualified "no." The fact that the spirits we experience on drugs seem good, nice, wise, thoughtful, and enlightening does not prove that they are not evil spirits, but good ones. In the biblical worldview, the whole point of temptation is that it always seems good, nice, wise, thoughtful, and enlightening. Think of the serpent in the garden. He thoughtfully challenged Eve. He used logic. He even opened her mind to try new experiences. Think about Satan tempting Christ (Matthew 4:1-11). He quoted scripture. He used logic. He offered to help. He provided new ways to get the things people wanted. Demons in the Bible rarely are scary. In fact, angels tend to be scarier than demons. When people in the Bible encounter angels they tend to fall down in fear.

Similarly, the fact that people who consume ayahuasca, LSD, and psilocybin report real benefits does not indicate the entities are beneficent. That creative people report better art, better tech inventions, and new ways of looking at life, or that people report healings from various ills (mental, emotional, and even physical) are not an indication, from a biblical perspective, that the entities are good. In fact, Christians throughout the ages would not be surprised by the claim that witchcraft brought tangible benefits. They might ask, isn't that the whole point of the "dark arts"? Would anyone practice magic if there was no upside? Isn't healing, knowledge, and power what it was always about?

No. Within the biblical/Christian worldview, neither warm feelings nor quantifiable benefits are proof that the spirits we encounter are good. So let us now step back and consider our Chapter 6 discoveries.

Everywhere in the world, there was a strange propensity for taking hallucinogens, worshiping serpents, and sacrificing innocents. Perhaps these themes are not coincidental. The Bible repeatedly warns about the conflation of the sacrificing of innocents and the use of drugs for spiritual purposes. What if there is something about the entities in the other dimension that gives them antipathy towards humans — especially the innocents? It all seems wild and mythical, but a simple review of both science and human history suggests that perhaps it's not.

It is with this in mind that the biblical warnings that at first seemed insane cease to seem so unhinged. Perhaps there is a real danger. Maybe the Bible is warning, with the strongest possible language, that when you practice pharmakeia you are meeting evil and very real entities that will indeed lead nations astray and provoke people to do unspeakable horror to the innocents among us. If true, the extreme reaction makes sense. *Don't use drugs for spiritual purposes because the spirits are demons.*

And with this in mind, let us look at some of the post-biblical Christian history as the church interacted with the dark arts.

VIII
Killing the Hydra

The Lernaean Hydra was a giant nine-headed water serpent. The Hydra terrorized whoever approached her, so Heracles was sent to destroy her. But every time he chopped off one of her nine heads, two more grew in its place. Heracles enlisted the help of his nephew Iolaus, and applied burning brands to the severed stumps. This cauterized the wounds and prevented them from growing back. It was only through this extreme effort that the serpent was finally stopped.

As Christianity transformed from a tiny, oppressed, minority religion to the official religion of the Roman Empire, a similar challenge confronted the missionaries working to expand the borders of Christendom. Pagan practices did not fade easily or quickly, but instead seemed to continually grow back. And as in the story of Heracles and the hydra, there were times in this era when efforts to destroy the serpent required extreme measures. Christians tore down temples, smashed idols, and illegalized pharmakeia.

The efforts to stamp out these pagan practices came early and often within Christian history. The great Saint Augustine of Hippo wrote in the fourth century, that "…all superstition of pagans and heathens should be annihilated is what God wants, God commands, God proclaims!"[152] And this strong statement was broadly accepted, taken seriously, and lived out by Christian communities throughout the Middle Ages.

In *The Darkening Age*, classicist Catherine Nixey dramatically recounts how "primitive" and "thuggish" Christians destroyed centuries-old pagan temples. Her account is harrowing. She writes:

> *"[When] the men entered the temple they took a weapon and smashed the back of Athena's head with a single blow so hard that it decapitated the goddess. The head fell to the floor, slicing off that nose, crushing the once-smooth cheeks. Athena's eyes, untouched, looked out over a now-disfigured face. Mere decapitation wasn't enough. More blows fell, scalping Athena, striking the helmet from the goddess's head, smashing it into pieces. Further blows followed.*

---

[152] Woodhead, 2004, 87.

The statue fell from its pedestal, then the arms and shoulders were chopped off. The body was left on its front in the dirt; the nearby altar was sliced off just above its base. Only then does it seem that these men — these Christians — felt satisfied that their work was done. They melted out once again into the desert. Behind them, the temple fell silent. The votive lamps, no longer tended, went out. On the floor, the head of Athena slowly started to be covered by the sands of the Syrian desert. The 'triumph' of Christianity had begun."[153]

This story, like so many that Nixey tells, paints the Christian forces as irrational zealots and the pagans as some innocent, peaceful crowd. In Nixey's mind, the reason the Christians were doing it is simple: the temple was "a monumental rebuke to monotheism."[154] Clearly, the efforts to end pagan worship were mostly just petty religious intolerance.

And the destruction certainly didn't stop with the temples. The insane-seeming effort to stamp out paganism from every corner of Christendom is the effort we now remember as "witch hunts." The Church, with various levels of intensity, pursued anyone that kept the old ways.

Many assume that when Rome officially converted to Christianity in the 4th and 5th centuries, the entire empire

---

[153] Nixey, 2018, XVII-XIX.
[154] Nixey, 2018, XVIII.

became Christian. In reality, the process of Christianizing Europe took much longer. Ireland was not Christianized until the 5th century. East Anglia (England) was not Christianized until the 7th. Bavaria (Germany) was also in the 7th century. And the Normans of France and Scandinavia didn't officially convert until the 10th and 11th centuries.[155] But "official" conversions didn't actually mean that the population became devout Christians. Often the "conversion" of the country was a political agreement on the part of a king or provincial ruler, used to build treaties with the Christians of southern and eastern Europe regarding war and trade. As with any religious transformation, the actual changing of the hearts of the people —the setting aside of the worship of the old gods and the practices of the old rites — lagged far behind these treaties. [156]

So, much of Europe (particularly the north) remained largely non-Christian until well into the second millennium AD. It is then not surprising that what we now describe as witch hunts did not gain steam until the late Middle Ages. Prior to this, official statements from the Church tended to be dismissive of witchcraft's capabilities and discouraged any sort of persecution of those accused of such practices.[157]Christian myths of the time depicting

---

[155] Holland, 2009, 179-187.

[156] See Stark, 2014, Chapter 13 for a nice overview of how religion spreads through societies after leaders convert.

[157] 906 AD: Regino of Prum, the Abbot of Treves, wrote the Canon Episcopi that reinforced the idea that witches had no real power while admitting that

missionaries killing dragons were not allusions to the actual killing of witches, but simply the putting-away of the serpent worship itself. The pagan people were largely spared physical violence from the Christians. In fact, in the early expansion of the Church, there were various statements from the Church explicitly prohibiting the killing of witches. For example, Charlemagne warned against the burning of witches in the eighth century saying, "If anyone, deceived by the Devil, shall believe, as is customary among pagans, that any man or woman is a night-witch and eats men, and on that account burn that person to death... he shall be executed."[158]

But as Christianity grew more established and pagan rites became less common, attitudes started to shift. It was not that witchcraft was absent before that, but that it was more accepted and normal. It was only when a large majority of the population and authorities had come to view the old religion as bad that efforts to stamp it out were made in earnest.

And they *were* made in earnest.

During the 16th and 17th centuries, a large number of people were executed for witchcraft.[159]The paganism that

some confused and deluded women thought that they flew through the air with the Pagan Goddess Diana. He assured readers that this was some form of hallucination.

[158] Hutton, 2017, 71.

[159] History Online, 2020.

remained in Europe now operated in secret. And like all secret religions, it was rumored to have evil practices. But the specifics of the rumors are interesting. In anti-witch literature such as the best-selling medieval tome *Malleus Maleficarum* and other popular accounts of witches at the time, witches were presented as pagans who worshiped Diana and other gods and goddesses, kidnapped babies, and killed and ate their victims.[160]

It is also interesting that during this period, the regions that had most recently converted to Christianity were those most likely to have high rates of witch hunts. Germany, for example, had the highest witchcraft execution rate, while Ireland —which converted early in the expansion of Christianity —had the lowest.[161] This would make sense if a significant and recent history of paganism remained within the living memory of the population.

Early in Christianity's growth, we saw an impassioned effort to bring down the pagan temples. Now that passion was turned toward anyone suspected of carrying on what once took place in those temples. There was a fear of the serpents whose images "teemed" on the walls of sanctuaries throughout the Roman Empire.[162] And the population knew these serpents came, not from buildings, but from the secret rites being performed within the buildings.

---

[160] Ankarloo, 2002, 5-9.
[161] History Online, 2020.
[162] Connelly, 2014, 46.

Muraresku does an excellent job of making the case that the witchcraft Christianity feared so much during the Middle Ages did indeed involve concerns about pharmakeia. He talks about how consuming an alternative form of Eucharist was a common theme in the witchcraft that Christianity tried so hard to stamp out. He discusses the work of a woman named Lucretia, who was prosecuted for practicing witchcraft.

"[So] many witnesses were asked to describe Lucretia's work with the 'ivy,' 'incense,' 'unguent,' and 'many herbs.'... It points to far higher sorcery and far deeper heresy. In the hands of a renowned witch who knew how to mix Dionysian ivy wine, spike incense with her own magical herbs, and fry up a lizard ointment, the body and blood of Jesus was a weapon. It fits Lucretia into a long line of heretics ... [and] potentially fits Lucretia into an even longer line of mystics who had been trafficking in a homemade Eucharist ever since the Gnostics."[163]

If we take witchcraft as secret efforts to carry on the pagan traditions within a recently converted population, then the idea that pharmakeia was involved is not a difficult conjecture. As we saw in Chapter 6, pharmakeia was the norm in many ancient religions.[164]

---

[163] Muraresku, 2020, 369.
[164] An interesting fact is that some scholars have speculated that the Salem Witch Trials may have been in part related to accidental poisoning with ergot, giving some of the people involved LSD-like psychedelic experiences. See Wilford,

And we see this explicitly in the writings of the Spanish explorers of the New World. Franciscan friar Fray Bernardino de Sahagún wrote:

> *"There is an herb named coatlxoxouhquij (green serpent), and it grows a seed they call ololiuquj. This seed produces inebriation and madness. People mix it in potions to give to those they wish to harm; those who eat it appear to see visions and terrifying things. Sorcerers mix it with food and drink..."*[165]

Notice the reference both to the serpent and to the visions that are seen. De Sahagún's observations were shared by the broader group of conquistadors who soon associated these visions with witchcraft. Juan de Cárdenas described the following:

> *"In sooth they tell us that peyote, and ololiuhque, when taken by mouth, will cause the wretch who takes them to lose his wits so severely that he sees the devil among other terrible and fearsome apparitions; and he will be warned (so they say) of things to come, and all this must be tricks and lies of Satan's, whose nature is to deceive, with divine permission, the wretch who on such occasions seeks him".*[166]

1976.
[165] Carod-Artal, 2015.
[166] Carod-Artal, 2015.

And we must remind ourselves that these are the very same people who were quite recently practicing widespread human sacrifice and other horrible acts at the time of this writing.

Now let's step back and review what we have learned so far. Those who practiced what the Bible calls pharmakeia saw visions of entities that even atheists today acknowledge might be real things. These entities come in many forms, but the serpent is one of them. This religion —what Brian Muraresku calls "the religion with no name"— has parallels found throughout the world. But darkly, these entities — especially the serpent — have a common request: the lives of innocents. Babies, children, and virgins.

Christian missionaries then followed the path of the mythical dragon slayers. They removed the pharmakeia and closed the mental portal to speak with the dragons. This caused the killing of innocents to end. Human sacrifice, so common throughout the ancient world, disappeared when the dragon was chained by Christian missionaries.

As one reads about the expansion of the Christian church throughout the world, one thinks of the passage toward the end of the biblical book of Revelation, where the writer discusses the epic chaining of the dragon and locking it away for "a thousand years."(Revelation 20:1-3)

When we think of medieval witch hunts we often think of some poor old lady who did nothing wrong being falsely accused by a bunch of uneducated religious zealots. The woman, we assume, was harmless, and the zealots had nothing to actually fear. They were being stupid. And even if she really did fancy herself a witch, who cares about some silly spell cast by a crazy old lady? But if we consider that perhaps in the living memory of some of these populations there was a real history of black magic with real cauldrons containing medicines that would bring the dragon who would then consume children, suddenly the fear doesn't seem quite as irrational.

Those "uneducated religious zealots" knew the danger of women mixing brews in the forest. They knew that the serpents seen by those who participated in pharmakeia would have dark demands. They knew that the entities were real. They knew of the other dimension. They had a legitimate fear of letting real evil reenter their world. Of things that had caused destruction in the past. They remembered children who had been killed by still-living grandparents to appease the gods. Temples of dragons that had been converted to churches still stood as a reminder.

Recently I read of an African bishop who was visiting Vancouver. Friends there had brought him to the popular tourist attraction, the Totem poles of Stanley Park. His friends were mortified when the Bishop started praying to exorcise demons from the poles and all who would worship them. When his friends asked him why he did it, he explained that he comes from a region where the danger of such religious practices is well known and the demons in the totems do real damage in the real world.

This seems very strange to our modern sensibilities because we have largely all agreed that demons are not real things. But everything we have learned so far about the observation of entities by sane and often quite skeptical people must cause us to rethink our skepticism. We cannot just dismiss the concerns of the bishop as superstition. Africa has, in living memory, seen tribes practicing human sacrifice as they sought to appease the entities that witchdoctors and shamans speak to while in trances.[167]

Of course, I am not justifying the witch hunts. Clearly many women and men were wrongly accused and prosecuted, and it is a very good thing that Christians recognized this error, put an end to witch hunts, and returned to the original and peaceful ways of slaying the dragon that the Church practiced in the early centuries of her operation. But what I am saying is that the seemingly insane reaction to the remnants of paganism in a recently-converted population might be more understandable

---

[167] Child Sacrifice in Uganda, 2011, 37.

than we often give credit for. In modern culture, we paint historical witches as sympathetic victims and the people trying to stop them as dull-witted oppressors, but we are likely getting these things reversed. A secret pagan ceremony in the woods was much more likely to be destroying an innocent person than a Christian church in the city square.

Furthermore, I propose that our current openness to pharmakeia may be a failure to cauterize a wound where one Hydra head has been lopped off. And where we fail to do this, perhaps the serpent will once again arise, stronger than ever, to impose damage and destruction on the innocents of this world.

The Christians of the Middle Ages remembered three things that we have forgotten: Drugs used for spiritual purposes. Serpent gods. And human sacrifice.

IX
The Dragon is Rising

There is a classic trope in horror movies that after the bad guy has been finally killed, the protagonist looks away, and— to the audience's horror — the bad guy rises again. As we reviewed in Chapter 1, there is a growing popular acceptance of pharmakeia in the West. We are seeing it adopted not by weird elderly women in the woods but by the rich, powerful and influential. It is not just accepted by hippies and social outsiders, but by the cultural mainstream. By academia. By Big Tech. And that acceptance is reflected in our changing laws.

The dragon is rising again.

How did Western Civilization go from being almost insane about destroying the serpent to cheering the serpent's return?

The use of psychedelics was reintroduced to the West in the 1950s and 1960s. LSD and psilocybin gained national prominence during the Harvard Psilocybin Project conducted by professors Timothy Leary and Richard Alpert. It was adopted by the counter-culture movement. Iconic bands like the Beatles, the Yard birds, the Grateful Dead, Jefferson Airplane, and Pink Floyd produced music with psychedelic themes, and their fans embraced this new experience. The Haight-Ashbury district near Berkeley, California became a hotbed for the use of LSD, and by the time of the historic Woodstock music festival in 1969, the use of LSD was widespread. It was so common that a theme at the concert was organizers and performers getting on the microphone to warn the crowd about a bad type of LSD that was circulating. But as quickly as the psychedelic craze rose, it began to fade again. The roots of its fall were present almost from the beginning.

In 1963, Timothy Leary was fired from Harvard after claims of chaos and hedonism taking place in his psilocybin "experiments" came to light publicly. And in 1965, he was arrested for possession of marijuana. In 1969, a concert at Altamont Speedway in Northern California — hoped by many to be the Woodstock of the west —descended into violence and death. The concert included the stabbing death of a young woman named Meredith Hunter, two deaths caused by a potentially drug-fueled accident, and one by

LSD-induced drowning in an irrigation canal. Many others were injured, and the concert was plagued by other crimes like car thefts and property damage. Also in 1969, murders committed by a hippie cult led by Charles Manson terrified the nation. These events and other scandals caused public opinion to turn sharply against the use of psychedelics.

In 1970, Nixon signed the Controlled Substances Act which, along with its subsequent amendments, placed strong penalties on the use of psychotropic drugs. Academic research on the effects of the drugs was strongly curtailed as well.

The concerns that led to this banning were primarily rooted in worries of this world and were not solely based on the religious considerations that drove the witch hunts of the late Middle Ages. Problems identified by medical experts of the day that have been confirmed with subsequent studies include persistent and lasting negative effects on the mental state of users (i.e., visual disturbances, disorganized thinking, paranoia, mood changes, and flashbacks).[168]

In addition, there was a general societal observation that people taking these types of drugs were more anti-social, that they rejected traditional family structures, and that they embraced lifestyles that older Americans viewed as undermining the very fabric of society. Parents saw their children having bad trips, acting erratically, and rejecting

[168] NIDA, Hallucinogens DrugFacts, 2019.

the religion and morals of the older generations. Divorce increased. Communist thinking increased. Satanic imagery came into vogue. And it became apparent to most people outside the psychedelic movement that the movement was a threat to society.

Another disquieting societal change that took place during this same period will echo themes from Chapter 6. The movement to allow the killing of the unborn through abortion in the USA took hold. The feminist movement, which had once opposed abortion, started to change during this era and the 1960s saw a major shift in attitudes toward abortion. State after state liberalized abortion laws. And then, in 1973, the Supreme Court established the legal right to access abortion nationwide. And the changes came from the same counter-culturalists who were using pharmakeia.

Interestingly, Margaret Sanger, the founder of Planned Parenthood (that has become the largest abortion provider in the United States) is said to have mapped out her strategy for the foundation of the institution with her mentor, Havelock Ellis, who is known to have been a user of psychedelics.[169]

Did the dragon still have a hunger for babies?

Another interesting development that took place during this time was a rejection of the one religion that had

---

[169] Grant, 1988, 57-58.

historically challenged the use of pharmakeia. One author describes the counter-culture movement of the 1960s and 1970s in the following way:

> *"The vast majority of hippies were young, white, middle-class men and women who felt alienated from mainstream middle-class society and resented the pressure to conform to the 'normal' standards …by wearing their hair long … taking drugs and exploring spirituality outside of the confines of the Judeo-Christian tradition, hippies sought to find more meaning in life—or at least have a good time."[170]*

I have noticed these same leanings among today's authors when it comes to their view of Christianity. As I have read some modern writers who favor the use of pharmakeia, they are almost uniformly hostile toward traditional Christianity. It jumps out of the page in the writings of Muraresku, Pollan, Hancock, and Gregory Sams.

In his essay, "Could Psychedelics Save the World," Sams writes:

> *"The powerful post-Constantine Church claimed a monopoly on spirituality, banning or destroying anything they thought to be in conflict with their religious hegemony."[171]*

---

[170] Pruitt, 2018.
[171] The Divine Spark: A Graham Hancock Reader: Psychedelics, Consciousness, and the Birth of Civilization, 2015, 300.

Here we see a theme that is present in the writings of other advocates of the use of psychedelics: Christians banned psychedelics as some sort of weird power move. Psychedelics were so great that the Church (which was boring and dry) had to ban them or lose its membership. Michael Pollan agrees and writes, speaking of drug-induced spirituality, "Mysticism...is the antidote to fundamentalism."[172]

Graham Hancock is also very outspoken in his criticisms of Christianity. For example, speaking of Christianity and other monotheistic religions he writes that they:

> "...exercise effective monopolies over the spiritual lives of more than half the world's population... All that is required to join the elect is to tick the right boxes and maintain a state of rigid, abiding, unquestioning BELIEF in the authority of the sacred texts and the utterances of the priests and mullahs self-appointed to interpret them."[173]

In Hancock's mind, the only reason Christianity could have for opposing pharmakeia is that it is in competition with pharmakeia. Christianity has a "placebo" Eucharist that doesn't actually take you to see the gods. But with pharmakeia, you see the gods directly and without assistance from the Church's power structure.

---

[172] Pollan, 37.
[173] Hancock G. , America Before: The Key to Earth's Lost Civilization, 2019, 478.

Another theme among pharmakeia proponents is that Christianity is the destruction of all great things ancient. Consider this passage from Muraresku's *Immortality Key*. Muraresku recounts a conversation he had with a scholar in Greece. The scholar expressed a frank assessment of Christianity's role in ending ancient pagan practices and Muraresku happily agrees, noting, *"This level of candor about Christianity's role in the death of classical civilization is rarely voiced back home, even among academics."*[174]

Even self-described Christians such as Mike Cernovich tend to be more open than the typical Christian to less orthodox forms of Christianity —Cernovich, for example, has promoted the spurious and Gnostic Gospel of Thomas (a work deemed heretical by the church and often embraced by critics of the church).[175]

In short, both in the 1960s and continuing to today, the rejection of orthodox Christianity has gone hand in hand with the acceptance of pharmakeia. The counterculture movement challenged the social bands — morality, tradition, and religion — holding American life together in the 1950s. And it raised concerns about safety, psychotic breaks, and the ability of users to contribute to society. So understandably, the response was strong and swift.

---

[174] Muraresku, 55-56.
[175] Tweet from Nov 3, 2021.

The Controlled Substances Act appeared to have conquered the dragon once again. But the victory was very short-term. The baby boomer generation, which participated in Woodstock and rocked out to The Beatles and the Stones, never quite agreed with the moral panic of their parents. Marijuana was largely not considered a big deal by them, and harder psychedelic drugs like LSD and mushrooms were not viewed with the same suspicion that previous generations had held. It is notable that the first baby boomer to become president of the United States, Bill Clinton, admitted to using marijuana.

Subsequent generations remembered the good things about the hippie movement (great music, cool concert art, and interesting thoughts on *expanded consciousness)* and were not taught about the violence and depravity that led their grandparents to fear it so much. As a result, as the children of the baby boomers began to rise to power there was little taste for strict enforcement of laws surrounding drugs viewed as minimally dangerous.

And slowly the questions started to move in the other direction. Why were minimally dangerous recreational drugs illegal? What was the big deal? Why lock people up for nonviolent crimes? Why was drug use a crime at all? And so we have seen the widespread legalization of marijuana and loosened laws on other hallucinogenic drugs like LSD and psilocybin. This indifference to the danger of hallucinogens is why Gen X and millennial commentators like Joe Rogan and Mike Cernovich speak about using psychedelics without embarrassment.

Which requires western civilization to make a decision: Do we fight the rising dragon once again?

X
St. George and the Way Forward

St. George has been charged with protecting the English royal family since the 14th century, and the Cross of Saint George is marked on the national flag of England. St. George saved the princess by marking the dragon with the sign of the cross. He led it like a dog into the city. He killed it when the townspeople converted to Christianity.

Western culture now stands at a fork in the road. Will we follow Saint George and once again subdue the dragon? Or will we free the dragon to do its will in the world?

Western Civilization appears ready to do the latter. Laws are loosening. Attitudes are softening. It seems like only a matter of time before we legalize ayahuasca, LSD, and mushrooms, and encourage their use as people see fit. After chaining the dragon for a thousand years, we appear to be ready to loose it once again.

Throughout this book, we have looked at pharmakeia and what happens when it is used by individuals and societies. We have acknowledged the potential benefits such as creativity, mental healing, and reduction of anxiety. And we have also noted the potential downsides such as societal disruption and mental and psychiatric harm. But we have also pointed to a much bigger concern: the possibility that the near-insane warnings of the ancients against pharmakeia as seen in the Bible and the legends of the Middle Ages are not in fact insane at all, but based on legitimate fears as to what the use of drugs for spiritual purposes can do to the world. We have asked the terrifying questions: What if — as both atheists and religious users of the drugs suggest — there are real entities that we are contacting when we consume these drugs? What if by changing our brain chemistry, we are able to perceive real beings in other dimensions not accessible while sober? And if this is the case, who are the entities? Who are the spirits? Are they malevolent or beneficent? When we look at the history of the world, we see that these entities all too often appear to inspire the worst in human beings.

Proponents of these drugs are quick to push back on the concept of banning them. One obvious pushback is that not everyone who takes these drugs interacts with serpents; as noted in Chapter 6, this is a common theme but not a universal one. Proponents will say that such visions are most common on DMT, and that other drugs such as psilocybin and LSD are more likely to only give visions of colors and geometry combined with an overall spiritual experience. They will state that the spiritual experience (entities and all) also offers benefits — the creativity and knowledge imparted are widely observed and used by cultures going back to the earliest days and continuing on to our own titans of technology.

So let us take a moment to weigh these benefits against the potential downsides, giving a fair hearing to the pushback of proponents before we conclude.

What benefits does the psychedelic experience offer? Let's evaluate this question from two perspectives: the moral/ethical effects and practical/power effects. These two considerations need to be looked at through both an individual and a societal lens— that is, how do these drugs affect individuals, and how do they affect societies?

Let's start with the practical. The evidence that we reviewed in chapters 2 and 3 may be enough to answer the question of practical benefits to the individual. Scientific studies (e.g., those performed by Johns Hopkins and New York Universities) demonstrate at least some promising therapeutic results. And perhaps the greatest benefit the psychedelic experience has provided is to music, the visual arts, and technology. The number of musicians who have experimented with drugs and produced creative and moving music as a result is almost too large to count. We can easily provide examples of great works by artists of the 1960s and 1970s such as The Beatles, Pink Floyd, and Led Zeppelin, who credited psychedelics with at least some of their brilliant art. And drug-positive artists such as Andy Warhol and Damien Hirst have also undoubtedly transformed the visual arts.

We can also point to figures such as Steve Jobs, who claimed that small amounts of psychedelics helped him with his creativity in the tech world. Other tech figures have claimed similar things, and there is no reason to doubt any of this. Further, as we look back on ancient societies that are known to have engaged in pharmakeia, we can observe similar brilliance. Both from an art standpoint — such as the beautiful psychedelic carvings on pyramids, and paintings on the walls of tombs — and from a technology standpoint. Consider the amazing accomplishments of Machu Picchu or Stonehenge. It becomes very hard to deny that pharmakeia could very well be contributing to the growth of art and technology.

On the other hand, many artists express a limit to the power offered by pharmakeia. For example, artists such as The Rolling Stones expressed embarrassment about their days doing psychedelics and consider their best music that which was produced after they had cut back a bit.

[176]Even the tech titans advocating the use of psychedelics typically promote "microdosing" — the practice of taking a very small amount of the drugs to limit the effects. And we all know people who got too into drugs and, rather than becoming creative geniuses, were ruined. Going back through the history of modern music and technology, for every John Lennon, we can name a Syd Barett (who was forced to leave Pink Floyd) or Brian Jones of the Rolling Stones (who was first kicked out of the band and then died due to drug and alcohol use).

For every musician or artist who has gained creativity or inspiration from drugs, we can point to the countless musicians who transformed music throughout the centuries with no apparent drug use. Whether classical musicians like Mozart or Beethoven or the newer styles of jazz, blues, country, or early rock 'n roll, many of the most influential musicians in history got their creativity naturally.

Further, looking at the question from the societal level — from a technology and knowledge standpoint — can we name a civilization that has become more advanced than the Christian West? The advancements of the medieval Gothic architects happened without drug use. The advancements of the Industrial Revolution happened without drug use. The advancements of electricity, the automobile, the telephone,

---

[176] Interestingly, Mick Jagger says that the album that was most messed up by psychedelic drugs was titled "Their Satanic Majesties Request." Taysom, 2021.

and the television all came without any apparent use of pharmakeia.

So when we look purely from a creativity and technological standpoint, the best we can say is that the use of pharmakeia brings mixed results. It can sometimes provide some benefits, but it is by no means necessary for creative leaps. And the most advanced society in known history happens to be the one that, inspired by Christianity, did the most to ban pharmakeia.

But it is important to also think about the fact that technology without morals or ethics is terrifying and bad. Chemicals can be used to make medicines, but they can also be used to make poisonous gas. Nuclear technology can be used to make cheap electricity, but it can also be used to blow up entire cities. The Germans of the early 20th century were one of the most advanced societies in the world but no one says, "thank goodness they were so advanced." No. Their use of technology to start two world wars and commit a holocaust caused us to recoil rather than to admire. For these reasons, our second question is much more important than our first: what are the moral and ethical effects on individuals and societies?

One of the big claims made by proponents of psychedelics is the supposed good effect they have on morals and ethics. Tripping causes a person to become more open, understanding, and tolerant of others, they say.

It helps us see our place in the universe and gives us a sense of unity with all creatures. Graham Hancock once opined that if all politicians would use ayahuasca, the world would be much better.[177] The drugs bring enlightenment to those that take them.

If this claim were true, it would certainly be a significant commendation for the legalization and use of psychedelics in western society. Unfortunately, it is also a very elusive and poorly supported claim. In fact, there is a notable *lack* of enlightenment among both societies and individuals. In their heads, people think they have become enlightened, but to those around them the signs of this enlightenment are often lacking.

A family member once told me a story about joining a commune back in the 1970s. The commune was comprised of good hippies who smoked a bit of dope and took a bit of acid and felt that a higher consciousness had been reached. About twenty of them went to live together on a farm in the mountains of Colorado. It was nice at first, but then it went downhill quickly. Some would work, others would not. Jealousy and weird relationship dynamics broke out. Someone started stealing firewood. And an unfortunate incident with a dog and chickens caused the dog's owner to almost come to blows with the owner of the chickens. The experiment lasted less than a year before it was over.

---

[177] Hancock G. , 2019.

And this is one of the most interesting things about pharmakeia. People claim to be enlightened by the experiences, but when you ask them what they learned, you get saccharine clichés about the oneness of everything and how we just need to love everyone. Not exactly enlightening.

This inability of users to share experiences or articulate lessons is notorious. As Michael Pollan writes:

> "Psychedelic experiences are notoriously hard to render in words; to try is necessarily to do violence to what has been seen and felt, which is in some fundamental way pre- or post-linguistic or, as students of mysticism say, ineffable. Emotions arrive in all their newborn nakedness, unprotected from the harsh light of scrutiny and, especially, the pitiless glare of irony. Platitudes that wouldn't seem out of place on a Hallmark card flow with the force of revealed truth."[178]

So we think we are being enlightened but we come out with Hallmark greetings?

No. People who regularly do psychedelics do not have stronger marriages or better relationships with their parents and children. They are not known for doing more charity work than sober people. It is hard to point to a single place where the users of psychedelics are more moral or ethical than the general population.

---

[178] Pollan, 251.

But as we saw in Chapter 6, saccharine platitudes and a lack of enlightenment are not the worst behaviors users of pharmakeia have exhibited through the centuries. Many societies that have used pharmakeia have done much, *much* darker things. When we look at the behavior of ancient societies such as the Aztecs or Celts, we can see that not only were they not enlightened, they were darkened to epic levels.

Societies that used pharmakeia practiced human sacrifice, infanticide, constant war, brutal xenophobia, and slavery. The Inca, whose priests used ayahuasca to direct their empire, also cut the hearts out of living children. If, as proponents of psychedelics often suggest, these drugs are the best hope for the enlightenment of humanity, why is it that when we actually look at societies that followed the guidance, it is unclear how things could have possibly been *less* enlightened?

And reviewing the history of Western society, the greatest reforms — the abolition of slavery, the creation of a welfare system for the poor, and the establishment of public hospitals — were all made by apparently very straight and sober (and often very Christian) reformers.[179] It is clear that drugs are not needed for real and sustainable societal reforms.

---

[179] See Ungit, 2021, Chapters 1, 2, and 3.

So as we step back and evaluate the moral and ethical effects of psychotropic drugs on individuals and society, we again are left wanting. The promises offered by proponents of the practice are completely missing. The drugs at best add no enlightenment or improved morals and ethics.

But what if psychedelics actively make morals and ethics worse? This is the question at the heart of this book. What if the death and destruction seen in so many societies throughout the world are at least in part being inspired by entities that we do not fully understand?

Entities from another dimension.

Entities that have entered the folklore of many religions.

Entities that do not have humanity's best interest in mind.

Even given the pushback that "not all psychedelics present us with entities," it can be countered that almost all psychedelic experiences are spiritual. And with every spiritual experience, the question can be asked: "which spirits?"

Western culture fought like hell to chain the pagan gods. They smashed pagan temples. They burned pagan idols. And most of all, they banned witchcraft — strange people in the woods mixing brews in big caldrons and practicing the dark arts. But after reading this book, I hope I have at least put the thought in the reader's mind that perhaps this fear was not as insane as is popularly conceived.

We saw in Chapter 4 that there is a real possibility that the entities and spiritual world observed while on psychedelics are more than mere hallucinations. We saw that even atheists, after trying them, agree that something real is there. We saw how these entities fit perfectly well within modern scientific conceptions of space-time and dimension. So the experiences while on drugs, the myths of old, and modern science might all be pointing to the same thing: a real realm containing real entities that can interact with us. Ancient religious categories called this dimension the heavenly dimension and the entities there were called gods, spirits, elves, angels, and demons. Modern atheists who observe similar entities call them inter-dimensional beings or aliens. But the question should not be what do we call them but instead: Who are they and what do they want?

As we saw in Chapter 6, the answer to this question might be very dark. These entities, often taking the shape of serpents, apparently have designs for human behavior that lead to the worst possible outcomes. They appear to have very negative influences on the societies that broadly accept them. We see that almost everywhere the serpent god was worshipped through the use of pharmakeia, he demanded the death of innocents. And this is why even dabbling in the use of these drugs or using methods to attempt to modulate or control the experience, such as 'microdosing' or using weaker drugs like pot, is so dangerous: the portal that is being opened may seem controllable, but if the entities are 'god-like' in power and knowledge can we really be so confident that our controls are effective?

We are so conditioned to view religion as a theoretical and possibly false thing that it is hard for us to get our minds around the idea that religious beings could actually enter our world. For this reason, the concept of another dimension within our universe is probably helpful, but we must consider that something exists that can be observed and interacted with by people in this world. Actual entities. Entities that have been observed across cultures. Entities even atheists recognize as real.

What if at least some of the old myths record real stories of real entities observed during some moment of altered consciousness in which the observers are able to see into the other dimensions? What if the warnings against the use of pharmakeia by the Bible and the historic Church are not the result of simple closed-minded, fun-spoiling bishops, but the result of the observation of something very real and very dangerous being very near to us all the time?

Michael Pollan tells the story of a dark and fascinating natural phenomenon. There is a mushroom that reproduces in a diabolical way.

The mushroom, *Cordyceps*, when consumed by an ant then commandeers the ant's body. The fungus causes the ant to climb a nearby plant and then causes the ant's head to explode, spreading spores out in the surrounding area. The mushroom commandeers the ant for its own purposes, which are very much to the ant's detriment. From everything we have reviewed, it is clear that mushrooms and other hallucinogens we take also have the potential to cause us to do things that are not in our own interest but instead are in the interest of some other entity.[180]

These findings sound shocking, and whenever I have brought them up to people who actually do these drugs I am met with a scoff. They immediately suppose I have never taken psychedelics (I have), and proceed to explain how neither they nor anyone they know has ever felt compelled to sacrifice a child to Moloch or any such thing. For them, their experience and that of a handful of friends disproves the dark claims made by the Bible, the witch hunters, and the present book.

And it is here that I must note an important point in this book. It is not my claim that all experiences while using drugs for spiritual purposes will lead to the absolute worst behaviors (murder of innocents). No. The point of Chapter

---

[180] Pollan, 89. Pollan didn't miss the parallel writing that, *"it occurred to me that Stamets[a psilocybin user he has met] and that poor ant had rather a lot in common. Fungi haven't killed him, it's true, and he probably knows enough about their wiles to head off that fate. But it's also true that this man's life—his brain!— has been utterly taken over by fungi..."*

6 and subsequent chapters is to point out that the spirits (whether in the form of entities or simply in the form of a spiritual experience) have clearly shown, at least at times, to **not have the best interests of humans in mind as they communicate with us**. This is a very important point that everyone needs to recognize. Saying, "I never felt compelled to murder children while on LSD," does not answer the question of whether the insights you gained while in that state would lead to your betterment and the betterment of those around you. We are so conditioned in modern society to assume that "spiritual" equals "good" that we never ask what ancients would have asked: "which spirit?"

When Eve encountered the serpent, she heard what he said and it sounded good to her. It sounded reasonable. It sounded beneficial. So she took the serpent's advice. In her case, we know the results and they were very bad. But what if the use of pharmakeia always takes us to see spirits — whether they come in the form of a serpent or not — that are tricksters, trouble makers, and human-haters? If this is the case then *all* advice from the spirits — all insights gained from these spiritual experiences — needs to be viewed with the highest levels of skepticism.

Michael Pollan interviewed participants from the Johns Hopkins psilocybin experiments and discussed the "insights" they had gained. Perhaps it is worth briefly looking at these insights and evaluating them skeptically. He tells the story of Amy, who got out of the experiment with a commitment to go into herbal medicine. Was that right for Amy? Would that lead her to happiness or fulfillment? We do not know, but can we at least be skeptical that this will not be a fix for her problems in life?

Even more interesting is that the "spiritual" experience gave her another conviction: to divorce her husband — to break her wedding vows and break up a family. The reason she gave was simple. She said, "my husband was late to pick me up....I needed him to be on time."[181] She decided to divorce her husband, not due to abuse or negligence, but because he was *tardy*? Was this a good decision? Was this a good spiritual insight that will be in her best interest or the interest of her husband? What if everyone followed this advice? Would this be good for families, for society, or for culture?

Other examples of spiritual insights that Pollan gave from the Johns Hopkins study include an unnamed psychologist who said that the spiritual experience taught her, "Trust, Letting go, Openness, and Being." Another participant named Richard said similar things. He said, "Our task in life consists precisely in a form of letting go of fear and expectations, an attempt to purely give oneself to the impact of the present."[182] This sort of Hallmark

---

[181] Pollan, 73.
[182] Pollan, 72.

greeting philosophy seems mostly innocuous, but what if that person, at that time needs to do the opposite? What if discernment is what is needed? What if forward-thinking is what is needed? We do not know the specifics of either of these people's lives, but the assumption that this advice is good advice depends very much on what sort of spirits are guiding their spiritual experiences.

Another participant Pollan interviewed, Brian, was guided to quit his job as a military contractor and to study Zen— eventually becoming a Zen monk.[183] Can we all agree that this is not the advice any of us would give a loved one? Was this good advice that was in his best interest? Is this the best way to make big decisions on important subjects such as religion and career? Again, only if you assume that all spiritual experiences are good experiences and that all spirits are good spirits. But if they are tricky, or worse, evil spirits, perhaps this advice is life- (or soul-) destroying advice? We can see that viewing spiritual insights with just a bit of skepticism changes their complexion. What seemed like insights or enlightenment could be foolishness or evil.

Further, it is important to consider the *type* of danger we are talking about. There are certain activities and behaviors that become more dangerous based on the number of people who adopt them. These are dangers that become pronounced only when they are participated in by a large

---

[183] Pollan, 73.

crowd (for example supporting fascism or communism). Pharmakeia has the potential of being this sort of danger. This matches what the ancient Hebrews said when they noted that pharmakeia "leads nations astray."[184]

And if this is the case, it matters *how* accepted the practice is. If it is relegated to a few strange individuals on the corners of society taking drugs in a van down by the river, it is unlikely that the broader society will be at risk or that any one individual will go far down the path of evil (although history certainly has its share of crazed drug-fueled crimes). But as more and more people accept the use of pharmakeia, the values and ideas given by the spiritual experiences will become normalized and accepted. As more and more people encounter the entities, will a twisted thirst for blood at a national level take hold? Remember how the psychedelic craze of the 1960s and 1970s was followed by a push to legalize abortion? And when centuries of acceptance pass, perhaps we will witness again the horrors seen among the Aztecs, the Inca, the Celts, and the Gauls.

We started this book by asking whether it was possible that a very early woman named Eve spoke to a serpent. And as fantastical as that sounded at the beginning of my research, we have seen that countless people (including atheists) claim it is very possible indeed to speak to a serpent. We've reviewed historical and contemporary testimonies of exactly

---

[184] Revelation 18:23.

this sort of experience. We've asked if it was possible that this serpent tempted Eve to do something forbidden, dark, and evil. Once again, this sounded fantastical at the beginning of this book but now it sounds like the same sort of request that the serpent deity has made of tribes and nations throughout the ages. And while the book of Genesis does not describe what the fruit was that Eve was tempted to consume — and it is possible that the fruit is an unimportant symbol of disobedience to the Divine in the story — we do know that a certain type of fruit (the many plants that can be eaten to see spirits) has been bound together with the serpent throughout the ages.[185]

Whether or not you take the story of Eve and the serpent to be literal is not the point of this book. The object of this book is to draw our attention once again to what the ancients knew — that pharmakeia and the dragon have always been bound up with destruction. We think we are more advanced than the ancients but what if — at least on this question — they understood things better than we do? The purpose of this book is to point to that message from Zeus warning not to open that box. The purpose of this book is to remind us of the victory of Saint George, and to humbly ask the reader to consider following in his footsteps.

---

[185] Brian Muraresku also sees the parallel between pharmakeia and the story of Eve, but paints it as a positive. He writes, "Back in the Garden of Eden, maybe the forbidden fruit was forbidden for a reason. Who needs the fancy building, the priest and all the rest of it—even the Bible—if all you really need is the fruit?" Muraresku, 36.

Appendix 1
What Are the Gnostic Gospels?

Every now and then someone confidently tells me that the early Church destroyed the real story of Jesus by burning and destroying alternative gospels. The belief is relevant to this book, as this is a common claim among those who suggest that original forms of Christianity did indeed practice pharmakeia. While this assertion usually comes with a lack of specificity, when pressed people will sometimes point to the "Gospel of Thomas" or one of the other "gospels" from the Nag Hammadi library. The Nag Hammadi library (also known as the "Gnostic Gospels") is a collection of texts discovered shortly after the end of the Second World War near the Upper Egyptian town of Nag Hammadi.

The Nag Hammadi discovery sent shock waves through the Western world, as scholars came to realize that the treasure of books represented an extensive amount of lost literature belonging to a group of early mystical and esoteric Christians declared to be heretical by Church fathers. It is thought that these books were buried in the wake of a declaration by 4th-century Church leaders, including Saint Athanasius, that the use of non-canonical gospels should be condemned.

Among the books of the Nag Hammadi library, the only complete work is known as the "Gospel of Thomas." The book is quite different from the gospels of the New Testament canon. Unlike those, it contains mostly a list of the sayings of Jesus, absent a narrative. And unlike the canonical gospels, Thomas avoids the often confusing debates that Jesus had about fine points of Jewish law, such as to what extent the Jews should obey their Roman rulers, and Jew/Gentile relations. Instead, the Jesus found in Thomas is one that speaks profound statements of religious truth encouraging his hearers to look within themselves for knowledge. "The one who seeks," Jesus says, "should not cease seeking until he finds."

Contrast this with the Jesus found in the four biblical gospels. We see him debating Pharisees on what is allowed on the Sabbath (Luke 6), debating whether Jews should pay taxes to Romans (Matthew 22), and making obscure rebukes to the regional ruler (Mark 8). We get a narrative that shows obscure locations around the region of Galilee and later Jerusalem. We hear specific names of Jewish people whose import has been lost to history. In short, when we think about what a holy book should look like, Thomas fits the part. Matthew, Mark, and Luke (and to a lesser degree John) don't.

This forces the question — was the Church right to reject Thomas (and the other Gnostic works) and keep the now-canonical gospels? Should they have kept them all? Do they contain helpful information about Jesus? By rejecting them, are we rejecting genuine historical information about Jesus?

The short answer is no. There are a number of good reasons we can be very confident, largely based on material within the canonical gospels, that the Gnostic gospels are later than the canonical gospels and are almost certainly a distortion rather than a clarification of actual first-century events.

Perhaps the number one "tell" that the Gnostic Gospels are a later and less accurate account of the life of Jesus is that they are distinctively pagan in their construction and make-up. Few scholars deny that Jesus and his earliest followers were Galilean Jews from the first century. And we know quite a bit about Jewish literature from this period.

We know that Jewish literature of this period was heavy on narrative. Consider some of the books now known as the Apocrypha such as Tobit (3rd century B.C.), 1 and 2 Maccabees (2nd century B.C.), and Judith (2nd century B.C.). And as we have seen, all four canonical gospels have a narrative form. We know that prior to the end of the first century the Jewish faith was centered on temple worship in Jerusalem. And we see the Temple at the center of many of Jesus' debates and controversies (consider Matthew 21, for example). And we can surmise that they would be interested in the politics and goings-on in the region. Again, we see exactly this in the four gospels of the New Testament - consider John the Baptist's ill-fated clash with the regional King Herod in Matthew 14.

Now contrast these features with what we have seen in the Gospel of Thomas. The narrative has been almost completely removed (it reads more like a series of wise aphorisms). Gone are the discussions on the temple. Gone are the discussions on the first-century controversies. Gone are the names of regional rulers and people of importance. Gone is the distinctively Jewish nature.

Now we must ask which is more likely? That distinctively Jewish accounts of Jesus would be taken and paganized as the faith spread from Israel to the pagans throughout the Roman Empire, or that a paganized account would be taken and made more Jewish in nature? The answer is obvious.

There are other reasons to be confident that Thomas is much later than the canonical gospels. For example, various verses are clearly redactions and harmonizations of the canonical gospels (sayings 10 and 16 in Thomas are clearly based on a harmonization of Luke 12:49, 12:51–52, and Matthew 10:34–35). Thomas followed these canonical texts because he bases his text on them.

And a final clue is that we have very early references to all four canonical gospels in Christian literature. By the mid-second century, we see all four of them being referred to and quoted. In contrast, we see no references to passages distinctive to Thomas or to the document as a whole.

So we can see that the early Christian church did not make a mistake in rejecting Thomas and the rest of the works found at Nag Hammadi. The Church had a standard for determining the canon of the New Testament: the works must either be authored by an apostle or have a very close connection with the apostles. For all the reasons we have reviewed above, the canonical gospels at least pass the smell test on this standard. They are closely connected to first-century Judaism in the region. And we see that there are very good reasons to suppose that the Gospel of Thomas and the other Gnostic works do not meet this standard; they were clearly compiled and composed by people separated by time, geography, and culture from the first-century Jewish world that Jesus and the Apostles were born into.

Appendix 2
The Problem of Consciousness

We humans are conscious. And we are conscious of the fact that we are conscious. The great Enlightenment philosopher and mathematician Rene Descartes put this at the very center of knowledge. Everything else could be questioned. I could be a butterfly dreaming that I am a human. But one thing I know: "I think, therefore I am." It is impossible to deny this without self-contradiction.

Because of our almost universal acceptance of naturalism, we are inclined to just assume that somehow physical things can become conscious. Humans are just moist computers (as Scott Adams says) and we became conscious. Therefore it follows that electronic brains might become conscious at some point as well.

But conceiving of how physical things might become conscious is an impossible thought experiment. Even hardened atheists like Richard Dawkins and Steven Pinker acknowledge the greatness of the problem. Dawkins writes (referencing Steven Pinker's work):

> "In How the Mind Works Steve elegantly sets out the problem of subjective consciousness, and asks where it comes from and what's the explanation. Then he's honest enough to say, 'Beats the heck out of me.' That is an honest thing to say, and I echo it."

Many laypersons do not see what Pinker and Dawkins see. For the average person, a computer is a sort of magical thing. We see a box with a bunch of circuit boards and wires in it that produces really cool outputs. Ask your iPhone to marry you and the voice comes back, "Let's just be friends." That is a witty and funny thing. Almost human. Siri will be conscious soon.

Except — no she won't. Wires and circuits are not magic, nor is well-written computer code.

Let me take away the "magic" of your iPhone with a helpful analogy an electrical engineering professor gave me. My undergraduate degree is in mechanical engineering and my university required me to take a couple of circuits classes just so I would not be totally ignorant. To explain to mechanical engineers how circuits worked, my professor suggested that we think of the flow of electrons through a circuit like water flowing through a complicated canal.

Voltage, he told us, can be thought of as the water level. Amperage could be thought of as the water speed. Resisters can be thought of as sharp bends in the canal. Switches can be thought of as a high wall that stops the flow of water. And motors can be thought of as a mill being turned by the flow of water. It was an imperfect analogy but it was helpful to understand what the various parts did.

But let's take that analogy further. Let's suppose we had the resources to construct a large network of canals. Let's suppose we could make the canals into a mechanical computer. Imagine switches and different paths through which the water can flow. We could create a computer code with the canals. If the water flows one way, it flips on a light. If it flows another way, it flips on another light. We could, with various water levels, bends, and forks, create a river that functioned as a simple computer. Give it inputs, and it would give outputs. It really is possible if you had a big enough canal and the workers to modify it.

Now — make that canal gigantic. Put it on some imaginary planet of almost infinite size (perhaps a Minecraft-sized planet) and cover it completely with canals. You could create a river supercomputer in which the flowing water flips lights on and hits speakers to make pre-programmed noises. You could make that river like Siri. It could make jokes. It could tell you the time. It could tell you the weather forecast.

But would that river and canal system ever be conscious? Of course not. It would just be water flowing through a canal, flipping on lights, and noise-making machines. However cleverly you designed the river, it would still be water running through canals. It would never, *never* be conscious. For that river to suddenly be able to think, "I am a river," would be something wholly un-mechanical. It would be magic. And rivers are not magic.

Neither are electrons.

It is not that we have not figured out the evolutionary step yet. It is that the step is in another dimension. It's outside the physical. It's a step into the spiritual dimension. This is why Dawkins and Pinker are stumped.

The fact that humans are conscious is a magical thing. It cannot be explained by evolution. It cannot be explained by physical processes. We are rivers of chemicals and electrons who are aware that we are rivers of chemicals and electrons.

After writing the above, I read "Conscious" by Annaka Harris. It is an interesting read and certainly worth checking out. I am not sure if Harris is an atheist or not, but her book certainly rejects any supernatural explanations for consciousness. Interestingly, she largely agrees with my criticisms of most naturalistic explanations for consciousness. She expresses reservations about the idea of consciousness coming as part of evolution, and even does a similar thought experiment to my mechanical computer analogy (using robots instead). But, as I said, as a committed naturalist, she also does not follow me that some sort of supernatural (non-atheist) solution must be appealed to.

Instead, she appears inclined toward an explanation called "panpsychism." Panpsychism is the idea that consciousness is not the result of evolution but instead is inherent in all matter. Every atom has some sort of awareness of being. She is careful to distinguish between a general consciousness and complex thought. A rock might have some level of awareness but, she would argue, it would take a brain (and the senses that come with the human body) to start forming any sort of complex thought. The rock might not think, "I am a rock," but it does have some sort of self-awareness. Everything does.

Harris argues that if panpsychism is true, then some sort of evolution of our consciousness is possible with the conscious and complex thought coming as the brain evolves and is able to process that inherent self-awareness into thoughts and ideas.

First, I want to say that I appreciate Harris's recognition of consciousness as the huge problem that it is for naturalists. I am continually surprised by how many people miss this and happily assume that complex systems/computers will inevitably become conscious. She knows this is faulty thinking.

I also wanted to express appreciation for her observation of how hard it is to tell if other things have consciousness. She notes the "zombie" thought experiment. In this thought experiment, imagine a robot or automaton that can act like humans (expressing grief over the passing of a friend and wonder at the beauty of the rising sun) that is simply following functions designed by its programmer. All the things we typically assume point to as evidence of conscious thought (a frown, a smile, a furrowed brow) are not actually signs of consciousness, but simply descriptions of behavior that happen to coincide with our own experience of consciousness. Consciousness is then completely unobservable and invisible to outside minds. The fact that other people have conscious thought cannot be proven. We have to take it for granted (i.e., I have consciousness thought so others must).

Finally, she does a great job of explaining how idiotic the idea of consciousness being an illusion is. This strange attempt to get around the problem does not work because an illusion is, by definition, something that deceives a conscious mind. Therefore *by definition,* the idea is flawed. Further, as she explains, the "consciousness is an illusion" solution doesn't answer any questions. Where did the illusion come from?

The book is helpful if for no other reason than to show the flaws of many of the traditional naturalistic arguments and explanations for consciousness.

But I would argue that Harris's attempts at providing her own solutions fall flat. Panpsychism is very problematic for reasons I will detail below. But before I do, I should also note that Harris is tentative with her endorsement of panpsychism. She says at various times that the goal of her book is more to ask questions than to provide solutions. At other times she seems open to some sort of combination of panpsychism and more traditional naturalistic explanations. But one thing she does not appear open to is any sort of traditional religious answer to the question. And I think that this problem will continue to be a problem until a religious solution – some idea of a God and some idea of a soul – is considered.

The case for panpsychism goes something like this:

1. We are conscious

2. This appears to be fundamental to who we are and cannot be explained by evolution

3. Therefore, if consciousness is inherent in ourselves, it might be (must be?) inherent in all things

It does not take a logician to see that #3 does not follow the premises #1 and #2. No. 3 can only be taken as an article of faith. Panpsychism is not the result of reason or logical deduction.

That doesn't mean it is not true, of course, but it does mean that we should not take it as a logical argument. It is possible that Harris is the only conscious thing in the universe. It is possible that there is no universe and that this is all her imagination. It is possible that she is a butterfly dreaming she is a human.

Like rationality, the existence of other souls (consciousnesses for the atheists out there) needs to be assumed. It cannot be proven.

A second problem with panpsychism is that it solves an incredibly mysterious problem with human existence by saying, "it was always there." I would argue that this is the scientific equivalent of creationism. Creationists believe that the complexity of the world was there at the beginning — that rather than being built by steps, God created it all in the beginning. Harris's argument is similar. This incredibly complex and mysterious thing that seems hard to build step by step can be explained by saying it was always like that. It is inherent.

Okay. Fine. Take that on faith. But explain to me why the Aristotelian or Platonic arguments for the existence of God are any less scientific.

Finally, the problem with panpsychism that is most commonly listed the combination problem. If consciousness is an inherent property of every atom (electron? proton? quark?), why does being close to another thing suddenly create one consciousness? Why would a dog be conscious (as a complete being), but not each individual atom of the dog (or each quark or whatever)? Why is it that if a human being loses a leg or an arm (part of our system), it does not appear to change our sense of consciousness?

Now, Harris does try to answer this in two ways. First, she speculates that maybe the areas of the human body that do not appear to be conscious (kidneys, for example) are conscious in some way but simply are unable to communicate it, and that our brains (being computers capable of complex thought and able to take in sensory input and express thoughts through language) are able to develop the complex thought and express it internally and through language. But this does not solve the combination problem. We still have constituent parts of the brain appearing to join together in a single consciousness.

She attempts to answer this more difficult question by suggesting that the problem lays with the illusion that consciousness and self are tied together. She references split-brain experiments in which, to stop seizures, patients had the two hemispheres of their brain separated and appeared to become two separate consciousnesses. The left hand would fight with the right hand. The left side would do something and the right side would (wrongly) explain why. Further, she discusses LSD experiments where people are conscious but lose their sense of self altogether. She then goes on to speculate that perhaps if you could meld two brains together that they might become a single consciousness. Without self-being attached to consciousness, she argues, the combination problem goes away.

This is an interesting effort, but it does not solve the problem. First, the hemisphere studies show behavior that might seem like two separate consciousnesses but, as she is good at pointing out, consciousness cannot be observed. So all we can say from these studies is that the patients displayed characteristics that typically would be associated with consciousness that appeared to be split. But to know for sure they were split, you would need to be that person. The person might have had one sense of consciousness that was malfunctioning in various ways. And the LSD studies might give the patients a feeling of losing their sense of self, yet their conscious thoughts did not actually combine with any other brain or any other being. In short, the experience reported is still a human being reporting something that they felt or sensed. It is a self-reporting feeling *self-less*.

But Harris's attempt to detach self from consciousness brings up a problem with much of what she has to say about consciousnesses as a whole. Her definition of consciousness is something quite different from what most people experience and know. Consider the following quote:

> *"Once again, it's important to distinguish between consciousness and complex thought when consider- ing panpsychic views. Postulating that consciousness*

is fundamental isn't the same as suggesting that com-
plex thoughts are fundamental and magically result
in a material realization of those ideas — a common
misinterpretation of panpsychism."

Rather than what we usually think of when we consider our own consciousness, she distills it down to the sense of "what it is like to be something."

But this is not what Descartes meant when he argued that the most fundamental element of knowledge was "I think therefore I am." This is not what we think of when we talk about our own minds. This is a definition that is quite distinct from what almost everyone means when we talk about consciousness. When we talk about our own mind, we are talking about self by definition. We are talking about the idea, "I am someone," that comes into our mind.

Harris's definition, even taken for what it is, does not explain how we get to "I am someone." She connects many little senses and says that somehow (thanks to being in a brain?) these become the complex thought, "I am someone." But it is this very question that we are looking for. How do we go from being electrons flowing through neurons to being a creature that says, "I am someone"? Panpsychism doesn't answer this question.

No thought experiment can bring these things together. And there is no way to measure or even observe them, as she perceptively explains. She ends her book by acknowledging that perhaps science is not equipped to give us the answers.

I commend her for this admission. I would argue that science cannot give us the answers. Something that she (rightly) admits cannot be observed, cannot be studied using a method that requires observation.

A Way Forward

Naturalism is not science. Science is a process of steps (hypothesis, experiment, analysis, conclusion). Naturalism is the assumption that there is no such thing as the supernatural and that what exists must be explained without reference to the Divine. However, historically, most scientists were not naturalists. And in the early days of science, almost all the scientists were committed Christians.

To say that something cannot be explained via natural processes, then, is not anti-science. Science requires observation, and as Harris convincingly argues, consciousness cannot be observed. That means that by definition the study of the soul must be moved from the scientific realm to the philosophical (or theological) realm.

With science, newer almost always equals better. The latest research is better to read than a study from fifty years ago. But with philosophy, the opposite is usually true. Philosophy depends on logical arguments and rational deduction. The longer a principle stands, the stronger it appears. Something that has stood the test of time is likely true — countless philosophers took shots at it and failed.

With this in mind, let's consider whether any old solutions to the problem of consciousness make sense. What about the religious idea of soul?

Harris dismisses this based on scientific research. We cannot have a soul, she says, because when we mess with the brain (via parasites, brain surgery, brain damage, etc.) weird things happen (our conscious understanding of our actions malfunctions and misinterprets and does other strange things). She even questions whether the conscious mind has any control over our actions at all (noting experiments that show our body knows we are going to do something before our conscious mind decides to do it).

This is an effective defeater of a particular understanding of soul. Specifically, this is an attack on Plato's idea of the ghost in the machine. Plato (with his shadows flickering in the cave) thought that matter was unimportant and evil — that the mind was fundamentally separate from the physical. To the extent that human minds are affected by the body, Plato argued, the effects are negative. The ideal state is disembodied bliss. Heaven, to Plato, was to lose your body and to be a free soul, unencumbered by the physical. But Harris notes that this view runs into major problems based on scientific experiments on the brain. Our conscious thought, far from being a ghost in the machine, appears to be part of the machine.

Harris uses this to dismiss the idea of a soul. But I wonder if she is aware that the Platonic view of the soul is not the Biblical view? The soul as seen in the Hebrew or Christian bibles is quite different. The biblical idea of soul is not one of a ghost in a machine. I highly recommend that Harris read N.T. Wright's *Surprised by Hope* to understand what the Bible says about body and soul. I should note here that her confusion is understandable, given that many Christians misunderstand this as well (so, everyone, please read Wright).

In *Surprised by Hope*, Wright (a retired Anglican Bishop and New Testament Scholar at the University of St. Andrews) explains that the Jewish/Christian hope has always been one of embodied existence. Humanity was created from matter (Genesis 1) and our final state will not be as ghosts but as resurrected (and embodied) humans on the last day (read 1 Corinthians 15). We worship a creator God (one who delights in the physical and even became physical himself). If there is a disembodied state at all, it is only for a very temporary period as saints wait for the final resurrection. Elsewhere, Wright argues that rather than a ghost in a machine, a better analogy is software on hardware. In *For All the Saints*, he quotes another bishop stating that when we die, "God will download our software onto his hardware until the day comes when he gives us new hardware on which to run our software once more."

If Wright's understanding of the soul is taken, Harris's critiques of the soul fall apart. Take a computer, mess with the hardware and the software will malfunction, wrongly diagnose, and otherwise do weird things. In short, we would act very much like the humans in the many studies she cites act. Our souls are not ghosts driving machines. Humans are integrated beings like computers. Our souls, like software, need hardware to work properly, and malfunctioning hardware messes with our software.

What about Harris's citing of studies that undermine free will? Well, it should be noted that many Christians (Reformed/Calvinists for example) deny the existence of free will also. Read the classic Jonathan Edwards work, *Freedom of the Will*, for an explanation of this view. Further, while the reformed view of the will maintains a freedom by placing it on the divine (God freely ordains), the naturalistic determinism that Harris's view would appear to mandate is philosophically untenable. If humans are simply mechanisms that respond to stimuli, then our thoughts cannot be considered rational at all and rational arguments must be illusory.

This creates a huge philosophical problem for naturalists, and is inherently nonsensical. There is no non-circular way to prove that our brains are rational. As soon as you start to provide rational reasons (arguments, logic, etc.) you are committing the logical fallacy of "petition principii" — assuming the thing you are trying to prove. For a system of thought to be rational, it cannot undermine rationality as something that can rightly be assumed. This is a problem for naturalism generally, but especially for any sort of deterministic naturalism.

So, the biblical view of soul appears to solve all the problems with consciousnesses. We are conscious because God gave us minds to know him. We are free to the extent that God made us free (and to the extent that we are not, he is). This is not a naturalistic solution. But it does not conflict with science, it is strong philosophically, and it lacks any fatal flaws.

Naturalism does not work for many reasons. Consciousness is just one of the most glaring holes.

Bibliography

Abortion Is Central to the History of Reproductive Health Care in America. (n.d.). Retrieved April 7, 2022, from Planned Parenthood: https://www.plannedparenthoodaction.org/issues/abortion/abortion-central-history-reproductive-health-care-america#:~:text=The%201960s%20gave%20rise%20to,Wade%20case.

Ankarloo, B. e. (2002). *Witchcraft and Magic in Europe, Volume 4: The Period of the Witch Trials.* United Kingdom: University of Pennsylvania Press, Incorporated .

Attala, L. (2011). Seeing Snakes and Vomitting. *ASA11*, (p. https://nomadit.co.uk/conference/asa11/paper/7171). University of Wales .

Austin, J. (2015, June 8). REVEALED: How ancient Philistines got WASTED on LSD-like drugs 3,000 years ago. Retrieved from Express: https://www.express.co.uk/news/weird/583018/ancient-Philistines-WASTED-LSD-drugs-3-000-years-ago

Biørnstad, L. (2020, September 15). *Researchers have examined the burial mound where the Gokstad Viking ship was found. What they found surprised them.* Retrieved from Science Norway: https://sciencenorway.no/archaeology-viking-age-vikings/researchers-have-examined-the-burial-mound-where-the-gokstad-viking-ship-was-found-what-they-found-surprised-them/1741928

Blakely, R. (2020, February 18). *Rampaging Vikings were fuelled by herbal tea.* Retrieved from The Times: https://www.thetimes.co.uk/article/rampaging-vikings-were-fuelled-by-herbal-tea-3mnpqq307

Brighenti, F. (2005). *Human Sacrifice in Ancient and Tribal India.* Retrieved from Svabhinava: http://www.svabhinava.org/friends/FrancescoBrighenti/Human-sacrifice.php

Broad, W. J. (2002, March 19). For Delphic Oracle, Fumes and Visions. Retrieved from New York Times: William J. Broad

Buckler, N. (n.d.). The Mysterious And Lost Magic Mushroom Rituals Of The Ancient Celts. Retrieved April 22, 2022, from The Old Moore's Almanac: https://oldmooresalmanac.com/the-mysterious-and-lost-magic-mushroom-rituals-of-the-ancient-celts/

Carod-Artal, F. (2015). Hallucinogenic drugs in pre-Columbian Mesoamerican culturesAlucinógenos en las culturas precolombinas mesoamericanas. *Neurología (English Edition)* , Volume 30, Issue 1, Pages 42-49.

Charbonneau, Jason . (n.d.). *DMT and Entity Encounters.* Retrieved April 3, 2022, from Think Anonymous: https://www.thinkanomalous.com/dmt.html

Child Sacrifice in Uganda. (2011). United States: Jubilee Campaign and Kyampisi Childcare Ministries.

Claffey, P. (2016, November 18). *A holy mountain: Croagh Patrick in myth, prehistory and history.* Retrieved from The Irish Times: https://www.irishtimes.com/culture/books/a-holy-mountain-croagh-patrick-in-myth-prehistory-and-history-1.2873508

Connelly, J. B. (2014). *The Parthenon Enigma.* United Kingdom: Knopf Doubleday Publishing Group.

Coulter-Harris, D. M. (2016). *Chasing Immortality in World Religions.* United States: McFarland, Incorporated.

Daley, J. (2016, August 12). *Did the Ancient Greeks Engage in Human Sacrifice?* Retrieved from The Smithsonian Online: https://www.smithsonianmag.com/smart-news/did-ancient-greeks-engage-human-sacrifice-180960111/

Davis, A., Clifton, J., Weaver, E., Hurwitz, E., & Johnson, M. G. (2020). Survey of entity encounter experiences occasioned by inhaled N,N-dimethyltryptamine: Phenomenology, interpretation, and enduring effects. *Journal of Psychopharmacology* , Volume: 34 issue: 9, page(s): 1008-1020.

de Voragine, J. (2012). *The Golden Legend: Readings on the Saints.* United Kingdom: Princeton University Press.

DMT Entities. (n.d.). Retrieved April 4, 2022, from DMT Times: https://dmttimes.com/dmt-entities

Doniger, W. (2009). *The Hindus.* United States: Penguin Press.

Dwyer, H., & Stout, M. (2012). *Aztec History and Culture.* Ukraine: Gareth Stevens Pub.

Dyck, E. a. (2020). Reframing Bummer Trips: Scientific and Cultural Explanations to Adverse Reactions to Psychedelic Drug Use. *The Social History of Alcohol and Drugs (posted by the University of Chicaggo Online)* , Vol 34 Number 2.

ed. John A Rush. (2013). *Entheogens and the Development of Culture: The Anthropology and Neurobiology of Ecstatic Experience.* United States: North Atlantic Books.

Editors of Encyclopaedia Britannica. (n.d.). *Wadjet.* Retrieved April 7, 2022, from Encyclopaedia Britannica: https://www.britannica.com/topic/Wadjet

El-Seedi HR, D. S. (2005). Prehistoric peyote use: alkaloid analysis and radiocarbon dating of archaeological specimens of Lophophora from Texas. Ethnopharmacol , 101 (1–3): 238–42.

Eschner, K. (2022, January 5). *The Promises and Perils of Psychedelic Health Care.* Retrieved from New York Times Online: https://www.nytimes.com/2022/01/05/well/psychedelic-drugs-mental-health-therapy.html

Evans, S. T. (2013). *Ancient Mexico & Central America : archaeology and culture history.* United Kingdom: Thames & Hudson.

Fenolio, D. B., & Crump, M. (2015). *Eye of Newt and Toe of Frog, Adder's Fork and Lizard's Leg: The Lore and Mythology of Amphibians and Reptiles.* United Kingdom: University of Chicago Press.

Feuer, W. (2020, November 4). *Oregon becomes first state to legalize magic mushrooms as more states ease drug laws in 'psychedelic renaissance'.* Retrieved from CNBC: https://www.cnbc.com/2020/11/04/oregon-becomes-first-state-to-legalize-magic-mushrooms-as-more-states-ease-drug-laws.html

Fridman, L. (2021). Rick Doblin: Psychedelics | Lex Fridman Podcast #202. USA.

Gibbons, J. (1998). Recent Developments in the Study of The Great European Witch Hunt. *The Pomegranate* , Issue #5.

Green, T. V. (2021, April 16). *Americans overwhelmingly say marijuana should be legal for recreational or medical use.* Retrieved from Pew Research Center: https://www.pewresearch.org/fact-tank/2021/04/16/americans-overwhelmingly-say-marijuana-should-be-legal-for-recreational-or-medical-use/

Griffiths RR, H. E. (2019). (2019) Survey of subjective "God encounter experiences": Comparisons among naturally occurring experiences and those occasioned by the classic psychedelics psilocybin, LSD, ayahuasca, or DMT. *PLoS ONE* , 14.

Griffiths RR, R. W. (2006). Psilocybin can occasion mystical-type experiences having substantial and sustained personal meaning and spiritual significance. *Psychopharmacology (Berl)* , 268-83, 284-92.

Grinspoon, D. H. (1979). *Psychedelic drugs reconsidered.* United States: Basic Books.

Hancock, G. (2019). *America Before: The Key to Earth's Lost Civilization.* United Kingdom: St. Martin's Publishing Group.

Hancock, G. (2019, April 22). JRE podcast #1284. (J. Rogan, Interviewer)

Hancock, G. (2016). *Magicians of the Gods: The Forgotten Wisdom of Earth's Lost Civilisation.* United Kingdom: Hodder & Stoughton.

Hancock, G. (2006). *Supernatural: Meetings with the Ancient Teachers of Mankind.* Ireland: Red Wheel Weiser.

Hancock, G. (2015). *The Divine Spark: a Graham Hancock Reader: Psychedelics, Consciousness, and the Birth of Civilization.* United States: Red Wheel/Weiser.

Hancock, G. (2022). *Visionary: The Mysterious Origins of Human Consciousness (The Definitive Edition of Supernatural).* United States: Red Wheel Weiser.

Harris, A. (2019). *Conscious: A Brief Guide to the Fundamental Mystery of the Mind.* United States: HarperCollins.

Harris, A. (2019, June 10). Making Sense #159 — Conscious. (S. Harris, Interviewer)

Hawking, S. (2010). *The Grand Design.* Italy: Bantam Books.

Hess, P. (2019, April 25). *Atheists Stopped Being Atheists After Taking Psychedelics.* Retrieved from Inverse: https://www.inverse.com/article/55228-atheists-stopped-being-atheists-after-taking-psychedelics

Hill, J. (n.d.). *Wadjet.* Retrieved April 7, 2022, from Ancient Egypt Online: https://ancientegyptonline.co.uk/wadjet/

Hillman, D. (2008). *The Chemical Muse.* New York: Thomas Dune.

History.Com Editors. (2020, October 20). *History of Witches.* Retrieved from History.Com: https://www.history.com/topics/folklore/history-of-witches

Holland, T. (2009). *The Forge of Christendom: The End of Days and the Epic Rise of the West.* United Kingdom: Knopf Doubleday Publishing Group.

Houston, J., & Masters, R. (2000). *The Varieties of Psychedelic Experience: The Classic Guide to the Effects of LSD on the Human Psyche.* United States: Inner Traditions/Bear.

Huels, E. R., Kim, H., Lee, U., Bel-Bahar, T., Colmenero, A. V., Nelson, A., et al. (2021). Neural Correlates of the Shamanic State of Consciousness . *Frontiers in Human Neuroscience* , VOLUME 15.

Hutton, R. (2017). *The Witch: A History of Fear, from Ancient Times to the Present.* United Kingdom: Yale University Press.

Jacobs, A. (2021, May 9). *The Psychedelic Revolution Is Coming. Psychiatry May Never Be the Same.* Retrieved from New York Times Online: https://www.nytimes.com/2021/05/09/health/psychedelics-mdma-psilocybin-molly-mental-health.html

Jaeger, K. (2021, June 1). *California Senate Approves Bill To Legalize Possession Of Psychedelics Like Psilocybin And LSD.* Retrieved from Marijuana Moment: https://www.marijuanamoment.net/california-senate-approves-bill-to-legalize-possession-of-psychedelics-like-psilocybin-and-lsd/

Jaekl, P. (2018, August 15). *Turns out near-death experiences are psychedelic, not religious.* Retrieved from Wired: https://www.wired.co.uk/article/near-death-experiences-psychedelic-religious

Jarus, O. (2017, June 17). *25 Cultures That Practiced Human Sacrifice.* Retrieved from LiveScience: https://www.livescience.com/59514-cultures-that-practiced-human-sacrifice.html

Johnstad, P. G. (2020). Psychedelic Telepathy: An Interview Study. *Journal of Scientific Exploration* , (3):493-512.

Kristinsson, J., & al, e. (2009). *Occurrence and Use of Hallucinogenic Mushrooms Containing Psilocybin Alkaloids.* United States: Nordic Council of Ministers.

Laurie, E. R., & White, T. (1997). Speckled Snake, Brother of Birch: Amanita Muscaria Motifs in Celtic Legends. *Shaman's Drum Journal* , no. 44.

Luke, D. (2022). Anomalous Psychedelic Experiences: At the Neurochemical Juncture of the Humanistic and Parapsychological. *Journal of Humanistic Psychology* , 62(2):257-297. doi:10.1177/0022167820917767.

Luke, D. (2018). What We Think We Know About DMT Entities. In *DMT Dialogues: Encounters with the Spirit Molecule* (p. 299). United States: Inner Traditions/Bear.

MacMullen, R. (1984). *Christianizing The Roman Empire A.D.100-400.* United States: Yale University Press.

Monmouth, G. o. (2009). *The History of the Kings of Britain: An edition and translation of the De gestis Britonum [Historia Regum Britanniae] (Arthurian Studies).* United Kingdom: BOYE6 .

Muraresku, B. (2020, September 30). Joe Rogan Experience Podcast #1543. (J. Rogan, Interviewer) Austin, Texas, USA.

Muraresku, B. (2020). *The Immortality Key: The Secret History of the Religion with No Name.* United States, : St. Martin's Publishing Group.

Narasimhan, S. (1992). *Sati: widow burning in India.* India: Doubleday.

National Geographic Staff. (2001, August 14). *Delphic Oracle's Lips May Have Been Loosened by Gas Vapors.* Retrieved from National Geographic Online: https://www.nationalgeographic. com/science/article/greece-delphi-oracle-gas-vapors-science

Nationalmuseet i København Staff. (n.d.). *Prehistoric period (until 1050 AD) / The Viking Age / Religion, magic, death and rituals / Human sacrifices?* Retrieved April 7, 2022, from Natmus: https:// en.natmus.dk/historical-knowledge/denmark/prehistoric-period- until-1050-ad/the-viking-age/religion-magic-death-and-rituals/ human-sacrifices/

Nixey, C. (2018). *The Darkening Age: The Christian Destruction of the Classical World.* United States: HarperCollins.

Owen, J. (2009, March 20). *Druids Committed Human Sacrifice, Cannibalism?* Retrieved from National Geographic Online: https://www.nationalgeographic.com/culture/article/druids- sacrifice-cannibalism

Pascal, M., Luke, D., & Robinson, O. (2021). An Encounter With the Other: A Thematic and Content Analysis of DMT Experiences From a Naturalistic Field Study. *Frontiers in Psychology* , Vol 12.

Pollan, M. (2018). *How to Change Your Mind: What the New Science of Psychedelics Teaches Us About Consciousness, Dying, Addiction, Depression, and Transcendence.* United States: Penguin Publishing Group.

Pomeroy, S. B. (1983). *"Infanticide in Hellenistic Greece" in Images of women in antiquity.* United States: Wayne State Univ Press.

Prince, M. A. (2019). Examination of Recreational and Spiritual Peyote Use Among American Indian Youth. Journal of studies on alcohol and drugs , 80(3), 366–370. https://doi.org/10.15288/jsad.2019.80.366.

Pruitt, S. (2018, September 14). *How the Vietnam War Empowered the Hippie Movement.* Retrieved from History.Com: https://www.history.com/news/vietnam-war-hippies-counter-culture

Razer, R. (2021). *Entities From The DMT Experience.* Retrieved from Entities From The DMT Experience: https://rafalreyzer.com/entities-from-the-dmt-experience/

Recht, L. (2020, February). *Human Sacrifice in the Ancient Near East and Egypt.* Retrieved from ASOR: https://www.asor.org/anetoday/2020/02/human-sacrifice/

Religion and Society in T'ang and Sung China. (1993). United States: University of Hawaii Press.

Reuters Staff. (2008, January 1). *Ancient Maya sacrificed boys not virgin girls: study.* Retrieved from Reuters Online: https://www.reuters.com/article/us-mexico-sacrifice/ancient-maya-sacrificed-boys-not-virgin-girls-study-idUSWRI32680820080123

Richards, W. (2018). *Sacred Knowledge: Psychedelics and Religious Experiences .* United States: Columbia University Press.

Romey, K. (2018, April 4). *Ancient Mass Child Sacrifice May Be World's Largest.* Retrieved from National Geographic Online: https://www.nationalgeographic.com/science/article/mass-child-human-animal-sacrifice-peru-chimu-science

Roos, D. (2018, October 11). *Human Sacrifice: Why the Aztecs Practiced This Gory Ritual.* Retrieved from History: https://www.history.com/news/aztec-human-sacrifice-religion

Saar, M. (1991). Ethnomycological Data from Siberia and Northeast Asia on the Effect of Amanita Muscaria. *Journal of Ethnopharmacology*, 157-173.

Salem Media. (2022, April 6). *Aztec Culture: How Many were Killed as Human Sacrifices?* Retrieved from History on the Net:

https://www.historyonthenet.com/aztec-culture-how-many-were-killed-as-human-sacrifices

Sfekas, S. (n.d.). *Aristotle's Concept of God*. Retrieved April 16, 2022, from HEPTAPOLIS: https://heptapolis.com/aristotles-concept-god

Shanon, B. (2002). *The Antipodes of the Mind: Charting the Phenomenology of the Ayahuasca Experience*. United Kingdom: Oxford University Press .

Sherman, J. (2015). *Storytelling: An Encyclopedia of Mythology and Folklore*. United Kingdom: Taylor & Francis.

Stark, R. (2014). *How the West Won: The Neglected Story of the Triumph of Modernity*. United States: Intercollegiate Studies Institute (ORD).

Strassman, R. (2000). *DMT: The Spirit Molecule: A Doctor's Revolutionary Research Into the Biology of Near-Death and Mystical Experiences*. United States: Bear.

Strassman, R. (2000). *DMT: The Spirit Molecule: A Doctor's Revolutionary Research Into the Biology of Near-Death and Mystical Experiences*. United States: Inner Traditions/Bear, 2000.

Strassman, R. J., Qualls, C. R., & Uhlenhuth. (1994). Dose-Response Study of N,N-Dimethyltryptamine. *American Medical Association Volume 51* , 98-108.

Sutter, P. (2021, July 8). *Can we explain dark matter by adding more dimensions to the universe?* Retrieved from Live Science: https://www.livescience.com/self-interacting-dark-matter-higher-dimensional-universe.html

Taysom, J. (2021, November 29). *The Rolling Stones album Mick Jagger said was ruined by "too many drugs"*. Retrieved from Far Out Magazine: https://faroutmagazine.co.uk/the-rolling-stones-album-mick-jagger-ruined-by-drugs/

The Divine Spark: a Graham Hancock Reader: Psychedelics, Consciousness, and the Birth of Civilization. (2015). United States, Red Wheel/Weiser, 2015.: Red Wheel/Weiser.

Tigg, G. R. (2013). *The Myth of Kukulkan*. United States: Wyatt-MacKenzie.

Timmermann, C., Roseman, L., Williams, L., Erritzoe, D., Martial, C., Cassol, H., et al. (2018). DMT Models the Near-Death Experience . *Frontiers in Psychology* , Vol 9.

Tolentino, C. (2022, January 16). *Snake Gods and Goddesses: 19 Serpent Deities from Around the World* , https://historycooperative.org/snake-gods-and-goddesses/. *Accessed January 19, 202*. Retrieved from History Cooperative: https://historycooperative.org/snake-gods-and-goddesses

Ungit, L. (2022, January 12). *Did the Early Church Use Psychedelics?* Retrieved from Notes from the Ungit: https://lewisungit.substack.com/p/did-the-early-church-use-psychedelics?s=w

Ungit, L. (2021). *The Emperoror Has No Clothes*. United States: Glome Press.

Vandette, K. (2022). *Native Americans were using psychoactive plants 1,000 years ago*. Retrieved from Earth: https://www.earth.com/news/native-americans-psychoactive-plants/

Vivot, R. M., Pallavicini, C., Zamberlan, F., Vigo, D., & Tagliazucchi, E. (2020). Meditation Increases the Entropy of Brain Oscillatory Activity. *Neuroscience* , 40-51.

Warmington, B. H. (1995). The Carthaginian Period. *General history of Africa, II: Ancient civilizations of Africa* , Vol. 2.

Wasson, R. G. (1967). Fly Agaric and Man. In e. D. Efron, *Ethnopharmacologic Search for Psychoactive Drugs,* (pp. 405-414). United Kingdom: Synergetic Press.

Wasson, R. G. (2021). *Soma Divine Mushroom of Immortality*. United States: Independently Published.

Wilford, J. N. (1976, March 31). *Salem Witch Hunts in 1692 Linked to LSD—Like Agent*. Retrieved from New York Times

Online: https://www.nytimes.com/1976/03/31/archives/salem-witch-hunts-in-1692-linked-to-lsdlike-agent-salem-witch-hunts.html

Wilson, L. (2001). *The Serpent Symbol in the Ancient Near East.* United States: University Press of America.

Wilson, P. L. (1999). *Ploughing the Clouds: The Search for Irish Soma.* United States: City Lights Publishers.

Woodhead, L. (2004). *An Introduction to Christianity.* United Kingdom: Cambridge University Press.

Wright, N. (2004). *For All the Saints: Remembering the Christians Departed.* United States: Church Publishing Incorporated.

Wright, N. T. (2008). *Surprised by Hope: Rethinking Heaven, the Resurrection, and the Mission of the Church.* United Kingdom: HarperCollins.

Zhang, M., & Campton, L. (2022, March 23). *How 'magic mushrooms' could follow in the footsteps of cannabis.* Retrieved from Politico: https://www.politico.com/news/2022/03/23/psychedelics-magic-mushrooms-cannabis-legalization-00016995